Foreword

This report examines the United States' foreign direct investment policies. It is the result of an examination held in February and October 1994 by an OECD Working Group made up of representatives of the Committee on Capital Movements and Invisible Transactions (CMIT) and the Committee on International Investment and Multinational Enterprises (CIME). These committees, whose members are officials from Ministries of Finance, Foreign Affairs, Commerce and Industry, and from central banks, promote liberal, non-discriminatory investment policies through the OECD Code of Liberalisation of Capital Movements and the National Treatment Instrument.

The report has been reviewed and adopted by both Committees and was derestricted by the OECD Council on 19 April 1995. Factual updating has been made through to the end of September 1994.

Table of contents

Chapter 3

General market access measures 53

Chapter 4

Sectoral measures 59

Annex 4

Introduction

As the largest recipient and source of foreign direct investment in the world, the United States occupies an important position in setting the multilateral framework for the treatment of foreign direct investment (FDI). Its large, robust and integrated market has attracted more foreign investment than any other country, while also providing US firms with a large base from which to invest abroad.

Direct investment patterns to and from the United States have changed over the last decade, with incoming investment – mostly in the form of acquisition of US firms – growing at an unprecedented pace in the late 1980s and making the United States a net importer of FDI during most of the decade. United States' firms expanded their investments overseas, too, with European countries taking in a larger share of the United States' FDI stock, and with outflows rising year-on-year during the early 1990s. Inward direct investment has responded to the renewed health of the economy, but outward investment remains stronger.

The United States has long supported the national treatment principle as a means to ensure that its investors are treated like national firms in foreign markets, and has generally applied this principle in its own laws and practices. With an ever-increasing foreign presence in the US market, and continued barriers to US investment abroad, and with the emphasis on promoting equal competitive opportunities for US firms abroad, pressures have grown to link the treatment of foreign firms in the US with the way US firms are treated overseas.

Notwithstanding these developments, the United States remains one of the most ardent proponents of an open international investment regime, and has played a key role in the effort to establish and implement multilateral commitments for the free flow of direct investment capital. FDI policy and practice in the United States is characterised by openness and non-discriminatory treatment of foreign investors, both those already established and those wishing to enter the

US market. No general authorisation is required for foreign direct investment in the United States, foreign investors are accorded fair, equitable and non-discriminatory treatment in most areas of economic activity, and exceptions to the national treatment principle are limited to specific sectors and certain federally-funded technology assistance programmes, USAID contracts and Federal Government air transport contracts.

This report examines the role of foreign direct investment in the United States, US direct investment policy as it has evolved in recent years, and impediments and conditions affecting direct investment. Chapter 1 analyses FDI trends in the United States and the role of foreign investment in the US economy. Chapters 2 to 4 examine the United States' FDI policies and practices, and Chapter 5 contains the study's conclusions. The United States current position under the OECD Capital Movements Code and National Treatment instrument are in Annex 1. Annex 2 summarises the Exon-Florio provisions. Annex 3 contains statistics on FDI in the United States. Annex 4 provides general statistics on FDI in the OECD area.

Chapter 1

The role of foreign direct investment in the United States' economy

A.   Overview

The United States is the largest source and recipient of foreign direct investment (FDI) in the world. The treatment of US multinational firms in foreign countries largely dominated US investment policy concerns for many years,[1] but in the early 1980's the United States became a net importer of FDI, and remained so during most of the decade. As a result, more attention has been given to inward direct investment issues. Even though outward direct investment has outpaced inward direct investment since 1991, FDI is reacting strongly to the economic recovery in the United States. The following trends stand out.

First, FDI inflows grew dramatically during the last decade, although with sharp fluctuations. From around $11.5 billion in 1983, they rose sharply between 1984 and 1989, reaching $69 billion in the latter year (See Table 1 and Chart 1). This represented 1.3 per cent of GDP and 7.5 per cent of domestic capital formation (Table 3 and Chart 3). From 1990-1992 FDI inflows declined substantially, barely reaching $3.4 billion in 1992, the lowest level recorded since 1975. As the growth of outward direct investment continued virtually unimpaired, the FDI balance turned negative – to $6.7 billion in 1991 and $33 billion in 1992. Direct investment from abroad recovered strongly in 1993, to $31.5 billion. This amount was nonetheless still $18.7 billion short of outward direct investment in that year.

Second, the United States has become the leading host country for foreign investment. In 1980, FDI stocks in the United States accounted for $83 billion, or 28.3 per cent of OECD countries' total FDI stocks (see Table 2 and Chart 2). In

11

Table 1. **Direct investment flows, 1973-1993**

US$ million

	Inward	Outward
1973	2 800	11 353
1974	4 760	9 052
1975	2 603	14 244
1976	4 347	11 949
1977	3 728	11 890
1978	7 897	16 056
1979	11 877	25 222
1980	16 918	19 222
1981	25 195	9 623
1982	13 810	1 078
1983	11 518	6 686
1984	25 567	11 649
1985	20 490	12 724
1986	36 145	17 706
1987	59 581	28 980
1988	58 571	17 871
1989	69 010	37 604
1990	48 422	27 705
1991	25 446	32 098
1992	3 388	37 122
1993	31 519	50 244

Source: Survey of Current Business, various issues.

Chart 1. **Foreign direct investment flows**
To and from the United States, 1973-1993

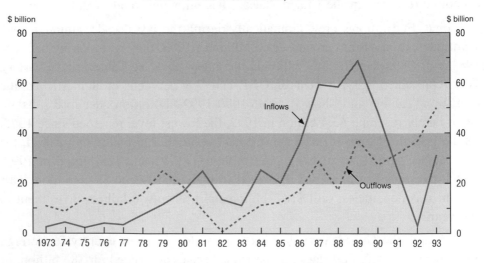

Source: OECD/DAF – Balance of payments data.

Table 2. **Direct investment stocks, 1973-1992**

US$ million

	Inward	Outward
1973	20 556	101 313
1974	25 144	110 078
1975	27 662	124 050
1976	30 770	136 809
1977	34 595	145 990
1978	42 471	162 727
1979	54 462	187 858
1980	83 046	215 375
1981	108 714	228 348
1982	124 677	207 752
1983	137 061	207 203
1984	164 583	211 480
1985	184 615	230 250
1986	220 414	259 800
1987	263 394	314 307
1988	314 754	335 893
1989	368 924	381 781
1990	394 911	426 958
1991	414 358	460 955
1992	419 526	486 670

Source: Survey of Current Business, various issues.

Chart 2. **Foreign direct investments stocks**

To and from the United States, 1973-1992

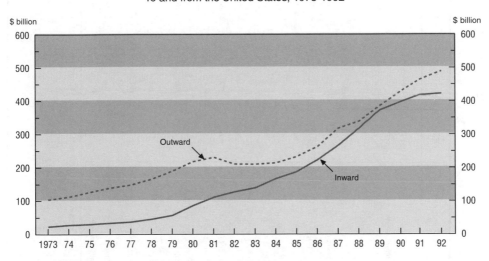

Source: OECD/DAF.

13

Table 3. Indicators of international direct investment, 1981-1993

US$ million

	1973-1980 average	1981	1982	1983	1984	1985	1986	1987	1988	1989	1990	1991	1992	1993
GDP	1 946 008	3 035 796	3 152 496	3 394 298	3 763 467	4 016 649	4 230 784	4 496 574	4 853 962	5 204 509	5 464 795	5 610 800	5 920 200	6 377 900
GDP nominal growth (%)	10.6	11.9	3.9	8.1	10.9	6.9	5.7	6.4	7.9	7.1	5.6	3.2	5.5	5.5
GDP real growth (%)	2.5	1.8	−2.2	3.9	6.2	3.2	2.9	3.1	3.9	2.5	1.2	−0.7	2.6	2.8
GFCF	381 642	603 834	590 658	626 364	727 809	782 985	807 866	829 874	886 860	920 556	920 587	862 478	912 900	876 100
CFCF growth (%)	..	58.2	−2.2	6.0	16.2	7.6	3.2	2.7	6.9	3.8	0.0	−6.3	5.8	−4.0
Inflows of FDI	6 866	25 195	13 810	11 518	25 567	20 490	36 145	59 581	58 571	69 010	48 422	25 446	3 388	31 519
Inflow growth (%)	..	266.9	−45.2	−16.6	122.0	−19.9	76.4	64.8	−1.7	17.8	−29.8	−47.4	−86.7	830.3
Inflows as % of GDP	0.4	0.8	0.4	0.3	0.7	0.5	0.9	1.3	1.2	1.3	0.9	0.5	0.1	0.5
Inflows as % of GFCF	1.8	4.2	2.3	1.8	3.5	2.6	4.5	7.2	6.6	7.5	5.3	3.0	0.4	3.6
Outflows of FDI	14 874	9 623	1 078	6 686	11 649	12 724	17 706	28 980	17 871	37 604	27 705	32 098	37 122	50 244
Outflow growth (%)	..	−35.3	−88.8	520.2	74.2	9.2	39.2	63.7	−38.3	110.4	−26.3	15.9	15.7	35.3
Outflows as % of GDP	0.8	0.3	0.0	0.2	0.3	0.3	0.4	0.6	0.4	0.7	0.5	0.6	0.6	0.8
Outflows as % of GFCF	3.9	1.6	0.2	1.1	1.6	1.6	2.2	3.5	2.0	4.1	3.0	3.7	4.1	5.7
Inflows − Outflows	−8 007	15 572	12 732	4 832	13 918	7 766	18 439	30 601	40 700	31 406	20 717	−6 652	−33 734	−18 725
Inf. − Out as % of GDP	−0.4	0.5	0.4	0.1	0.4	0.2	0.4	0.7	0.8	0.6	0.4	−0.1	−0.6	−0.3
Outflows/Inflows (%)	2.2	0.4	0.1	0.6	0.5	0.6	0.5	0.5	0.3	0.5	0.6	1.3	11.0	1.6

Source: US Department of Commerce, Survey of Current Business; OECD: National Accounts of OECD Countries; OECD Economic Outlook.

Chart 3. Inflows of FDI as a percentage of GDP and GFCF
1981-1993

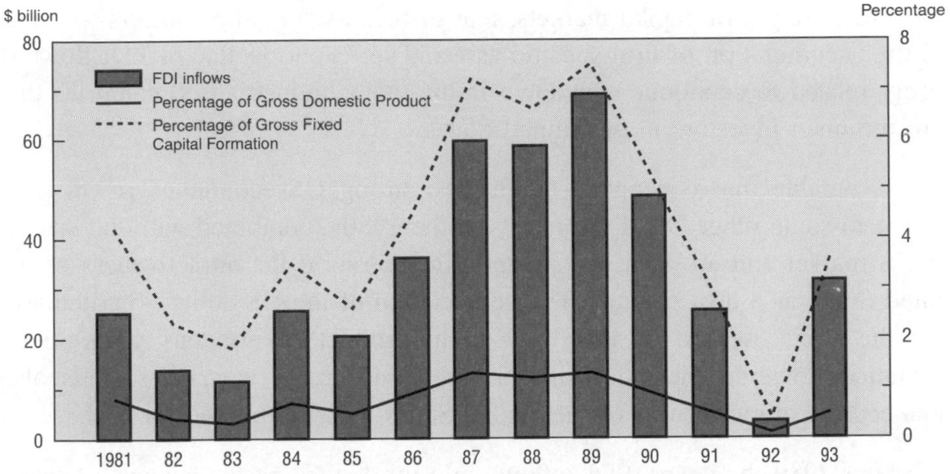

$ billion / Percentage

Legend:
- FDI inflows
- Percentage of Gross Domestic Product
- Percentage of Gross Fixed Capital Formation

Source: OECD/DAF.

1992, this figure increased to $419.5 billion, or 35.9 per cent of OECD countries' FDI stocks. This sharp rise took place as world FDI was expanding on an unprecedented scale.

Third, FDI inflows into the United States mostly took the form of acquisitions of existing firms rather than greenfield investments. This pattern was particularly strong in the second half of the 1980s (see Table 3). In 1986, acquisitions accounted for $31.4 billion as opposed to $7.7 billion for greenfield operations (see Annex 3, Table 1). The value of FDI through acquisitions was almost five times greater than that of greenfield investments between 1986 and 1989. Acquisitions also seem to have been the preferred mode of entry since the 1993 recovery.

B. Causes of FDI surge and decline in the 1980s and early 1990s

The surge and decline of FDI inflows in the last decade resulted from a combination of factors. According to reports prepared by the US Department of

15

Commerce and other studies,[2] the major reasons for the rise in FDI in the United States can be grouped under four headings: macroeconomic conditions, world-wide liberalisation of capital markets, fear of increased market barriers to entry, and the accumulation of firm-specific assets. The recent decline of FDI flows is closely related to economic slowdown in the major industrialised countries that were the main investors in the United States.

Favourable macroeconomic conditions: strong US economic growth rates relative to some other OECD countries in the 1980s, combined with the size of the US market and an open investment climate, raised the attractiveness of the United States as a host country. The depreciation of the US dollar – particularly after the Plaza Accord in 1985 – as a by-product of previous years' trade imbalances lowered the value of US assets in foreign currencies. This also enhanced the attractiveness of the United States as a destination for FDI.

After 1989, however, FDI inflows into the United States began to decline sharply because of a slowdown of economic growth in the major investing partners such as the United Kingdom and Canada, coupled with the heavy investment requirements of the German unification and asset deflation in Japan.

The liberalisation of capital markets created favourable conditions for the financing of FDI. In the 1980s, industrialised countries, including the United States, United Kingdom, Japan, France, and Italy, undertook substantial deregulation of domestic financial markets and cross-border capital transactions.

Threats of entry barriers in the US markets, such as import restrictions and voluntary export restraints, seem to have induced strategic acquisitions and establishment of US facilities in several US industries by foreign multinational enterprises. This factor played a particularly important role in Japanese investments in the United States, particularly in the automotive sector.[3]

Finally, the development of firm-specific assets in other industrialised countries also helps to explain the surge of FDI inflows into the United States.[4] In the 1950s and 60s, US-based firms maintained superiority over foreign-based firms in many firm-specific assets, such as technology, management skills and financial resources. The existence of such firm-specific assets led US firms to exploit these advantages in foreign countries.[5]

European and Japanese firms, too, developed their own specific advantages during the process of post-war economic recovery and reconstruction. Combined with an increase in available funds, these firms have been able to reap the benefits from these accumulated assets by investing in the United States. And the superiority of US firms declined in relative terms in the 1970s and 1980s. This is considered one the most fundamental reasons for the surge of FDI inflows in the 1980s.

C. FDI inflows

i) Countries of origin

FDI from OECD countries has become more and more important in the United States during the last decade. FDI inflows from OECD countries expanded rapidly, particularly in the last half of the 1980s, when the percentage share of FDI stocks held by OECD countries increasing from 85.1 per cent in 1983 to 93.3 per cent in 1992 (Table 4 and Chart 4).

Five countries – the United Kingdom, Japan, the Netherlands, Canada and Germany – have been the major investing countries in the United States. Together, they accounted for 76.6 per cent of total FDI stocks in the United States in 1992. Europe as a whole accounted for 52 per cent of these stocks, Latin America and Caribbean countries for 4.5 per cent and the Middle East for 1.1 per cent and South and South East Asia for 0.9 per cent.

The United Kingdom maintained its leading position until 1991 and even increased its share slightly – from 23.5 per cent of total FDI in 1983 to 24.2 per cent in 1991. However, Japan surpassed the United Kingdom in 1992 because of the very large investments it made during the second half of the 80's. In fact, Japan's FDI stock increased more rapidly than any other country, with its share of total US FDI stocks rising from 8.3 per cent in 1983 to 23.1 per cent in 1992.

FDI from OECD countries into the United States decreased sharply after 1989 under the influence of the world recession and other factors, such the heavy debt created by earlier by-outs and excess capacity in the United States market, and special factors in source countries, notably the cost of German unification

Table 4. **Foreign direct investment: position at year-end by country, 1981-1992**

In US$ million

	1981	1982	1983	% of total	1984	1985	1986	1987	1988	1989	% of total	1990	1991	1992	% of total
OECD AREA	**92 489**	**105 064**	**116 637**	**85.1**	**142 074**	**160 529**	**196 791**	**245 594**	**293 902**	**341 909**	**92.7**	**366 607**	**387 478**	**391 218**	**93.3**
Europe	72 006	82 853	92 839	67.7	108 566	120 748	144 085	180 842	208 844	239 126	64.8	247 253	251 065	248 224	59.2
EEC	64 354	74 300	82 493	60.2	97 231	106 820	127 220	161 059	188 342	212 361	57.6	220 874	223 548	219 134	52.2
Belgium-Luxembourg	2 173	2 240	2 558	1.9	3 301	2 636	2 750	3 961	3 340	4 206	1.1	6 095	4 026	4 609	1.1
France	5 876	5 708	5 726	4.2	6 591	6 670	7 709	10 137	13 233	15 365	4.2	18 650	24 155	23 808	5.7
Germany	9 459	9 850	10 845	7.9	12 330	14 816	17 250	21 905	25 250	28 386	7.7	28 232	28 618	29 205	7.0
Ireland	130	132	219	0.2	285	.	360	544	725	1 416	0.4	1 340	1 823	2 273	0.5
Italy	829	1 120	1 238	0.9	1 438	1 237	1 323	1 310	752	1 436	0.4	1 524	2 705	571	0.1
Netherlands	26 824	26 191	29 182	21.3	33 728	37 056	40 717	46 636	48 128	56 734	15.4	64 671	59 355	61 341	14.6
Spain	201	273	194	0.1	231	273	350	442	511	601	0.2	792	1 155	1 290	0.3
United Kingdom	18 585	28 447	32 152	23.5	38 837	43 555	55 935	75 519	95 698	103 458	28.0	98 676	100 386	94 718	22.6
Other Europe	7 652	8 553	10 346	7.5	11 335	13 928	16 865	19 783	20 502	26 765	7.3	26 379	27 517	29 090	6.9
Sweden	1 693	1 739	2 124	1.5	2 258	2 357	3 963	4 910	4 713	5 435	1.5	5 484	5 684	6 923	1.7
Switzerland	5 474	6 378	7 464	5.4	8 146	10 568	12 058	13 772	14 372	18 746	5.1	17 674	19 189	19 562	4.7
North America	12 116	11 708	11 434	8.3	15 286	17 131	20 318	24 684	26 566	30 370	8.2	29 544	37 301	38 997	9.3
Canada	12 116	11 708	11 434	8.3	15 286	17 131	20 318	24 684	26 566	30 370	8.2	29 544	37 301	38 997	9.3
Other OECD Countries	8 367	10 503	12 364	9.0	18 222	22 650	32 388	40 068	58 492	72 413	19.6	89 810	99 112	103 997	24.8
Australia	572	730	930	0.7	2 125	3 264	5 466	5 369	7 171	4 962	1.3	6 542	6 083	7 140	1.7
Japan	7 697	9 677	11 336	8.3	16 044	19 313	26 824	34 421	51 126	67 268	18.2	83 091	92 896	96 743	23.1
NON OECD AREA	**16 225**	**19 613**	**20 424**	**14.9**	**22 509**	**24 086**	**23 623**	**17 800**	**20 852**	**27 015**	**7.3**	**28 304**	**26 880**	**28 308**	**6.7**
Africa	18	13	3	0.0	3	4	9	521	441	505	0.1	505	643	635	0.2
Latin America-Caribbean	11 739	14 229	15 035	11.0	16 201	16 826	16 763	10 103	11 243	16 218	4.4	20 168	17 665	18 895	4.5
Argentina	149	130	194	0.1	237	280	292	305	291	370	0.1	420	371	403	0.1
Brazil	110	100	84	0.1	160	201	182	293	286	428	0.1	377	478	502	0.1
Mexico	163	259	244	0.2	308	533	847	293	218	350	0.1	575	708	1 184	0.3
Middle East	3 588	4 401	4 446	3.2	5 336	4 954	4 870	4 973	6 570	7 588	2.1	4 425	4 771	4 813	1.1
Israel	312	428	449	0.3	525	494	567	632	587	630	0.2	640	1 147	1 131	0.3
Saudi Arabia	247	370	353	0.3	425	420	436	257	1 826	2 455	0.7	1 811	1 598	1 642	0.4
South and South East Asia	296	486	685	0.5	1 065	1 118	1 574	2 018	2 540	2 656	0.7	3 158	3 638	3 734	0.9
DAEs	194	372	550	0.4	896	917	1 387	1 814	2 353	2 356	0.6	2 833	3 334	3 411	0.8
Hong Kong	169	229	324	0.2	659	640	605	941	895	1 124	0.3	1 511	1 763	1 714	0.4
Korea	−103	−55	−57	−0.0	−81	−101	383	198	505	−307	−0.1	−1 009	−618	−496	−0.1
Singapore	26	97	186	0.1	208	242	169	391	510	934	0.3	1 289	870	847	0.2
Taiwan	74	80	69	0.1	70	107	177	199	329	476	0.1	836	1 142	1 154	0.3
Other Asia	102	114	135	0.1	169	201	187	204	187	300	0.1	325	304	323	0.1
Philippines	77	102	116	0.1	121	118	113	73	73	82	0.0	77	54	59	0.0
Other Countries	584	484	236	0.2	−146	1 134	355	94	−33	−36	−0.0	. .	1	. .	0.0
TOTAL	**108 714**	**124 677**	**137 061**	**100.0**	**164 583**	**184 615**	**220 414**	**263 394**	**314 754**	**368 924**	**100.0**	**394 911**	**414 358**	**419 526**	**100.0**

Source: United States Department of Commerce, Bureau of Economic Analysis: *Survey of Current Business,* various issues.

Chart 4. **Foreign direct investment: position at year-end by country**

1992

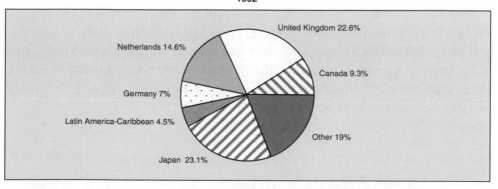

United Kingdom 22.6%

Netherlands 14.6%

Canada 9.3%

Germany 7%

Latin America-Caribbean 4.5%

Other 19%

Japan 23.1%

1989

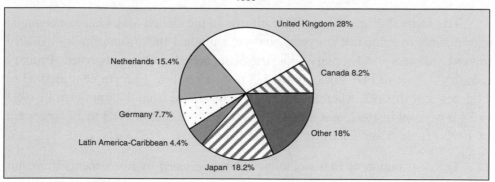

United Kingdom 28%

Netherlands 15.4%

Canada 8.2%

Germany 7.7%

Latin America-Caribbean 4.4%

Other 18%

Japan 18.2%

1983

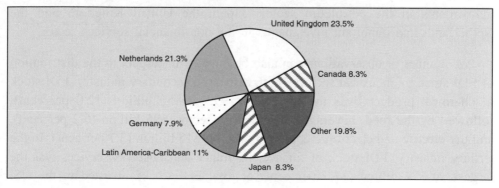

United Kingdom 23.5%

Netherlands 21.3%

Canada 8.3%

Germany 7.9%

Latin America-Caribbean 11%

Other 19.8%

Japan 8.3%

Source: OECD/DAF.

and the fall of Japanese equity markets. In fact, in 1992, FDI inflows from European countries and Canada was outpaced by US FDI into these countries, so the balance ended up being negative (–$46 million and –$2 144 million, respectively). FDI inflows from Japan dropped from $10.7 billion in 1991 to $4.0 billion in 1992. The OECD investors' share of total FDI into the United States came down from 91.8 per cent in 1989 to 70.6 in 1992. While detailed statistics are not yet available, these figures need to be assessed against the surge of FDI activity in 1993 (see Annex 3, Table 2, Chart 1).

ii) Sectoral distribution

The sectoral distribution of FDI inflows to the United States has not changed significantly over the last ten years, and yet a gradual shift from primary industry toward secondary and tertiary industries can nonetheless be observed. Primary industry's share of FDI stocks in the US decreased from 15.5 per cent in 1983 to 11.5 per cent in 1992, whereas secondary's increased from 34.8 per cent in 1983 to 38.0 per cent in 1992, and tertiary's from 49.7 per cent in 1983 to 50.5 per cent in 1992 (Table 5 and Chart 5).

The distribution of FDI stock has been dominated by investments in manufacturing, trade, and financial services (banking, finance and insurance). Some countries, notably the United Kingdom and the Netherlands, also had significant investments in the petroleum sector. Japan, the United Kingdom and the Netherlands had important investments in the non-financial services sector.

A number of observations can also be made with respect to the distribution of FDI stock by industrial sectors. With respect to secondary industry, FDI stock in chemical products was the largest in 1992 at $50 billion (12.0 per cent), followed by the food, beverages and tobacco sector, $25 billion (6.2 per cent), and the electric and electronic equipment sector, $15 billion (3.7 per cent). In the tertiary industry, FDI stock of finance, insurance and business services was the largest, at $74 billion (17.7 per cent) of total FDI stocks invested in the US, followed by the wholesale and retail trade sector, at $66 billion (15.8 per cent). (See also Annex 3, Table 3 and Chart 2).

Table 5. **Foreign direct investment: position at year-end by industry, 1981-1992**

In US$ million

	1981	1982	1983	% of total	1984	1985	1986	1987	1988	1989	% of total	1990	1991	1992	% of total
PRIMARY	**18 346**	**20 584**	**21 285**	**15.5**	**30 470**	**33 415**	**35 424**	**44 656**	**44 562**	**46 436**	**12.6**	**52 825**	**49 419**	**48 084**	**11.5**
Agriculture	948	1 043	1 148	0.8	1 150	1 106	1 250	1 250	1 116	1 350	0.4	1 457	1 107	1 058	0.3
Mining and quarrying	2 152	1 876	1 928	1.4	3 920	4 039	5 080	5 591	7 440	4 741	1.3	8 486	8 116	8 481	2.0
Oil [1]	15 246	17 660	18 209	13.3	25 400	28 270	29 094	37 815	36 006	40 345	10.9	42 882	40 196	38 545	9.2
SECONDARY	**40 533**	**44 065**	**47 665**	**34.8**	**51 802**	**59 584**	**71 963**	**93 865**	**122 582**	**150 949**	**40.9**	**152 805**	**156 586**	**159 492**	**38.0**
Food, beverages and tobacco [2]	5 722	6 639	7 448	5.4	8 270	10 710	12 147	15 506	16 458	23 585	6.4	22 543	23 773	25 898	6.2
Textiles, leather and clothing [3]	455	352	491	0.4	412	440	747	1 169	2 075	2 873	0.8	1 785	1 616	1 349	0.3
Paper, printing and publishing	2 881	3 207	3 622	2.6	3 748	4 467	6 270	6 637	11 509	12 836	3.5	14 662	13 935	13 924	3.3
Chemical products	13 701	14 377	15 756	11.5	16 631	18 836	22 954	26 291	30 926	38 408	10.4	45 746	48 414	50 255	12.0
Coal and petroleum products	..	..	..	..	..	..	..	..	..	..	..	..	..	..	..
Non-metallic products [4]	403	480	621	0.5	834	774	1 353	2 230	4 003	4 323	1.2	5 580	5 831	6 499	1.5
Metal products	4 449	5 178	5 322	3.9	5 893	6 952	7 282	7 824	10 873	15 110	4.1	13 713	13 164	13 182	3.1
Mechanical equipment	3 656	3 526	3 408	2.5	3 812	3 916	4 349	5 099	9 273	12 762	3.5	11 527	11 473	10 936	2.6
Electric and electronic equipment	4 641	5 069	5 200	3.8	5 871	5 318	7 198	10 628	13 179	15 077	4.1	16 099	17 111	15 445	3.7
Motor vehicles	652	991	1 328	1.0	1 302	1 899	1 919	1 519	2 012	3 736	1.0	3 100	2 938	2 722	0.6
Other transport equipment	341	516	328	0.2	578	459	579	1 275	780	1 052	0.3	548	1 030	1 114	0.3
Other manufacturing	3 632	3 730	4 131	3.0	4 451	5 813	7 165	15 687	21 494	21 187	5.7	17 502	17 301	18 168	4.3
TERTIARY	**49 834**	**60 027**	**68 110**	**49.7**	**82 311**	**91 617**	**113 028**	**124 874**	**147 610**	**171 537**	**46.5**	**189 280**	**208 353**	**211 950**	**50.5**
Construction	3 152	3 692	3 676	2.7	4 337	4 037	3 602	1 345	1 519	2 407	0.7	4 110	3 842	2 135	0.5
Wholesale and retail trade	20 537	23 604	26 513	19.3	31 219	35 873	42 920	45 399	53 590	54 005	14.6	60 152	64 347	66 203	15.8
Transport and storage	905	1 135	1 255	0.9	1 226	1 459	1 797	1 790	1 994	2 221	0.6	2 285	2 248	1 493	0.4
Finance, insurance and business services	15 204	18 645	20 460	14.9	43 812	27 429	34 978	44 883	51 499	66 226	18.0	59 728	72 672	74 069	17.7
Communication	198	244	317	0.2	..	383	397	159	52	−86	−0.0	1 062	1 045	1 407	0.3
Other services [5]	9 838	12 707	15 889	11.6	..	22 436	29 334	31 298	38 956	46 764	12.7	61 943	64 199	66 643	15.9
UNALLOCATED	**1**	**1**	**1**	**0.0**	..	..	..	**−1**	..	**2**	**0.0**	..	..	..	..
TOTAL	**108 714**	**124 677**	**137 061**	**100.0**	**164 583**	**184 616**	**220 415**	**263 394**	**314 754**	**368 924**	**100.0**	**394 910**	**414 358**	**419 526**	**100.0**

1. Including petroleum manufacturing products and petroleum related services.
2. Excluding tobacco which appears under "Other manufacturing".
3. Excluding leather which appears under "Other manufacturing".
4. Including rubber and other plastic products.
5. Including real estate, hotels and restaurants, motion pictures, engineering, accounting and other services.
Source: United States Department of Commerce, Bureau of Economic Analysis: *Survey of Current Business,* various issues.

Chart 5. **Foreign direct investment: position at year-end by industry**

1992

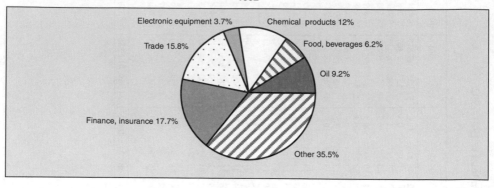

1989

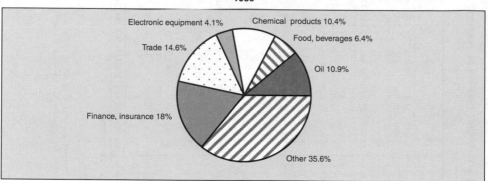

1983

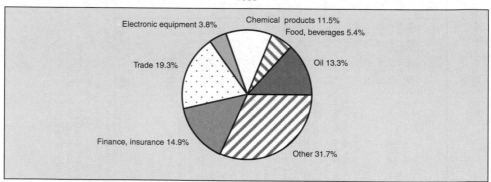

Source: OECD/DAF.

D. Impact on the US economy

i) Output, capital formation, productivity and R&D

Given the fact that the United States had not been a major host country until the 1970s and also because of its size, the involvement of foreign-owned companies in the US economy has been rather modest. The surge of FDI inflows has changed this situation in a number of respects, however. These changes appear to derive mainly from the shift of ownership from US to foreign firms – as opposed to growth in the operations of the firms themselves. Empirical evidence does not enable a clear determination of the incremental economic benefits from foreign ownership. Keeping in mind these considerations, the following observations can be made from the data.

Non-bank affiliates of foreign-owned companies accounted for 2.6 per cent of total US GDP in 1980, and this figure rose to 4.6 per cent in 1990. From 8.0 per cent in 1980, US foreign-owned firms in the manufacturing industry increased their contribution to gross domestic product to 14.0 per cent in 1990 (Annex 3, Table 4).

Employment in non-bank foreign-owned companies also increased significantly. While they employed two million workers (or 2.7 per cent of total US employment) in 1980, this figure had almost doubled in 1990, to 4.7 million workers, or 5 per cent of total employment (Annex 3, Table 5). In manufacturing, the role of foreign-owned companies has become even more significant. While they accounted for 5.4 per cent of manufacturing employment in 1980, this figure was around 11 per cent in 1990. US affiliates also appear to have paid higher wages.

New plant and equipment expenditures made by non-bank foreign-owned companies increased from 5.5 per cent of total US new plant and equipment expenditures in 1980 to 12.2 per cent in 1990 (Annex 3, Table 4).

Foreign investors have also contributed to US technological capability and development. While still small, their share of US high-technology industries is rising. They are also slightly more concentrated in high-technologies industries than are US-owned firms. Non-bank foreign-owned companies made 15.4 per cent of total US research and development (R&D) expenditures in 1990 as compared to 6.4 in 1980 (Annex 3, Table 4).

Using value-added as a proxy for productivity, foreign-owned companies' performance would also appear to have been higher than that of total US companies although the gap also seems to have become smaller.

ii)   Imports, exports and trade balance

US affiliates of foreign-owned firms were heavily involved in international trade throughout the 1980s, and continue to be today. In 1990, they accounted for 23.2 per cent of total US exports and 30.9 per cent of total imports. Imports of foreign-owned firms increased rapidly from $245.3 million in 1980 to $495 million in 1990, despite the US dollar's depreciation after 1985 (Annex 3, Table 6). The trade deficit of foreign-owned companies expanded drastically in the 1980s – from $23.6 million in 1980 to $89.5 million in 1990. This amounted to 88 per cent of the US total trade deficit that year.

Foreign firms were not only more dependent on imported inputs than US-controlled firms, but they also mainly sourced these inputs from their parent firms. Their merchandise imports from these firms rose sharply from $47.0 billion in 1980 to $136.7 billion in 1990. The increase was particularly accentuated in the second half of the 1980s.

A number of sectoral differences may nevertheless be observed. Foreign firms' ratio of imports to sales was relatively lower than the average (15 per cent) in manufacturing industry (11.6 per cent), and relatively higher in wholesale industry (29.7 per cent). The motor vehicles and equipment industry showed the highest import dependence overall (34.1 per cent for manufacturing and 48.5 per cent for wholesale) (Annex 3, Table 7). The import dependence of Japanese-owned companies was the highest among foreign-owned companies.

E.   FDI outflows

i)   Countries of destination

While the growth of US FDI outflows was less spectacular than FDI inflows during the second half of the 1980's and its share of OECD outward stock actually declined from 51 per cent in 1981 to 29 per cent in 1991, the United States remained the largest investor in the world. US investment overseas even

Table 6. Direct investment abroad: position at year-end by country, 1981-1992

In US$ million

	1981	1982	1983	% of total	1984	1985	1986	1987	1988	1989	% of total	1990	1991	1992	% of total
OECD AREA	NA	**152 246**	**153 870**	**74.3**	**155 911**	**170 897**	**192 978**	**236 219**	**251 644**	**285 741**	**74.8**	**322 956**	**345 459**	**352 967**	**72.5**
Europe	NA	92 449	92 178	44.5	91 589	105 171	120 724	150 439	157 077	186 109	48.7	212 728	232 428	237 912	48.9
EEC	NA	74 339	72 717	35.1	71 844	83 898	98 624	123 999	131 069	158 864	41.6	179 101	197 662	200 535	41.2
Belgium-Luxembourg	NA	6 647	5 644	2.7	5 008	5 728	5 808	7 927	8 342	9 270	2.4	11 096	12 389	12 634	2.6
France	NA	7 391	6 614	3.2	6 406	7 643	8 952	11 868	13 041	16 443	4.3	18 950	20 798	23 257	4.8
Germany	NA	15 463	15 319	7.4	14 823	16 764	20 932	24 388	21 832	23 673	6.2	27 480	34 027	35 393	7.3
Ireland	NA	2 031	2 460	1.2	2 869	3 693	4 308	5 425	5 886	4 665	1.2	5 725	6 635	7 229	1.5
Italy	NA	4 316	4 461	2.2	4 594	5 906	7 426	9 264	9 496	11 221	2.9	14 076	14 775	13 605	2.8
Netherlands	NA	6 760	6 613	3.2	5 839	7 129	11 643	14 842	16 145	19 160	5.0	18 720	19 772	19 114	3.9
Spain	NA	2 350	2 287	1.1	2 139	2 281	2 707	4 076	4 966	6 500	1.7	7 802	7 992	8 165	1.7
United Kingdom	NA	27 537	27 637	13.3	28 553	33 024	35 389	44 512	49 459	67 722	17.7	72 343	78 072	77 842	16.0
Other Europe	NA	18 110	19 461	9.4	19 745	21 273	22 100	26 440	26 008	27 245	7.1	33 627	34 766	37 377	7.7
Norway	NA	2 735	3 094	1.5	2 841	3 215	3 216	3 843	4 371	3 447	0.9	4 209	4 349	4 047	0.8
Switzerland	NA	12 863	14 099	6.8	14 725	15 766	16 441	19 665	18 734	21 144	5.5	25 151	25 604	28 662	5.9
North America	NA	43 511	44 339	21.4	46 730	46 909	50 629	57 783	62 656	63 948	16.7	69 106	68 853	68 432	14.1
Canada	NA	43 511	44 339	21.4	46 730	46 909	50 629	57 783	62 656	63 948	16.7	69 106	68 853	68 432	14.1
Other OECD Countries	NA	16 286	17 353	8.4	17 592	18 817	21 625	27 997	31 911	35 684	9.3	41 122	44 178	46 623	9.6
Australia	NA	9 089	9 005	4.3	8 918	8 772	9 340	11 363	12 823	14 368	3.8	14 997	15 795	16 697	3.4
Japan	NA	6 407	7 661	3.7	7 936	9 235	11 472	15 684	18 009	19 911	5.2	22 511	24 938	26 213	5.4
NON OECD AREA	**NA**	**55 506**	**53 333**	**25.7**	**55 569**	**59 353**	**66 822**	**78 088**	**84 249**	**96 040**	**25.2**	**104 002**	**115 496**	**133 703**	**27.5**
Africa	NA	6 486	6 110	2.9	5 896	5 891	5 516	5 869	5 471	3 936	1.0	3 592	4 442	3 518	0.7
Latin America-Caribbean	NA	28 161	24 133	11.6	24 627	28 261	36 851	47 551	53 506	62 145	16.3	70 752	76 214	88 860	18.3
Argentina	NA	2 864	2 702	1.3	2 753	2 705	2 913	2 744	2 597	2 215	0.6	2 479	2 767	3 353	0.7
Brazil	NA	9 290	9 068	4.4	9 237	8 893	9 268	10 591	12 609	14 025	3.7	14 268	14 882	16 114	3.3
Mexico	NA	5 019	4 381	2.1	4 597	5 088	4 623	4 913	5 712	8 264	2.2	10 255	12 257	13 330	2.7
Middle East	NA	3 550	4 451	2.1	5 025	4 606	4 891	4 084	3 806	3 518	0.9	4 007	4 823	5 814	1.2
Saudi Arabia	NA	1 495	2 156	1.0	2 352	2 442	2 460	2 092	1 782	1 655	0.4	1 772	2 163	2 503	0.5
South and South East Asia	NA	12 142	13 039	6.3	15 045	15 400	15 332	17 010	18 528	19 836	5.2	22 980	27 398	32 246	6.6
DAEs	NA	7 809	8 140	3.9	8 819	8 876	9 918	11 549	12 940	15 522	4.1	17 370	21 047	24 997	5.1
Hong Kong	NA	2 854	3 068	1.5	3 253	3 295	3 912	4 389	5 240	5 412	1.4	5 994	6 516	8 544	1.8
Korea	NA	690	589	0.3	716	743	782	1 178	1 501	2 370	0.6	2 677	2 862	2 779	0.6
Singapore	NA	1 720	1 821	0.9	1 932	1 874	2 256	2 384	2 311	2 998	0.8	3 183	5 294	6 631	1.4
Thailand	NA	780	892	0.4	1 081	1 074	1 078	1 274	1 132	1 511	0.4	1 789	2 038	2 459	0.5
Other Asia	NA	4 333	4 899	2.4	6 226	6 524	5 414	5 461	5 588	4 314	1.1	5 610	6 351	7 249	1.5
Indonesia	NA	2 295	2 770	1.3	4 093	4 475	3 217	3 070	2 921	2 771	0.7	3 175	3 783	4 278	0.9
Other Countries	**NA**	**5 314**	**5 721**	**2.8**	**5 204**	**5 428**	**4 448**	**3 782**	**3 184**	**6 917**	**1.8**	**3 040**	**2 839**	**3 002**	**0.6**
TOTAL	NA	**207 752**	**207 203**	**100.0**	**211 480**	**230 250**	**259 800**	**314 307**	**335 893**	**381 781**	**100.0**	**426 958**	**460 955**	**486 670**	**100.0**

Source: United States Department of Commerce, Bureau of Economic Analysis: *Survey of Current Business*, various issues

Chart 6. **Direct investment abroad: position at year-end by country**

1992

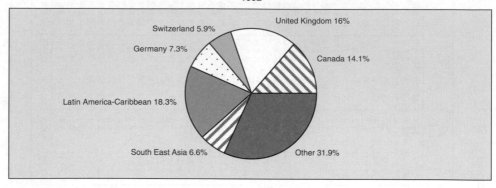

1989

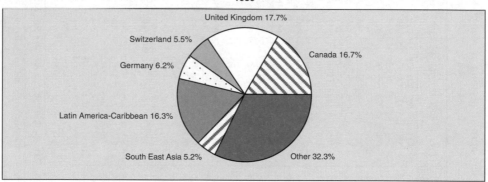

1983

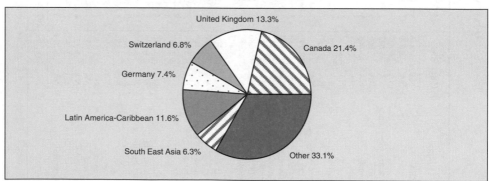

Source: OECD/DAF.

picked up in the midst of the world recession in 1991 and 1992 and was stimulated more by the 1993 recovery. It fluctuated around 0.6 per cent of US GDP and 4 per cent of domestic capital formation during the period (Table 3). The main countries of destination were the United Kingdom, followed by Canada and Germany. The US FDI stock in the UK was $77.8 billion, or 16 per cent of the total, Canada was $68.4 billion (14.1 per cent), and Germany was $35.3 billion (7.3 per cent) in 1992 (Table 6, Graph 6).

Some changes in the traditional geographical patterns of US outward investment can be observed. Europe picked up an even greater share of US outward stock, from 35 per cent in 1983 to 41 per cent in 1992, partly as a result of liberalisation there. The percentage of Latin American and Caribbean countries increased from 11.6 to 18.3 per cent (or some $88.9 billion). And Japan's and the Dynamic Asian Economies' shares increased from 3.7 per cent and 3.9 per cent in 1983 to 5.4 per cent and 5.1 per cent in 1992, respectively. On the other hand, Canada's share decreased sharply from 21.4 per cent in 1983 to 14.1 per cent in 1992 (see also Annex 3, Table 8).

ii) Sectoral distribution

Although FDI outflows did not grow as rapidly as FDI inflows in the last decade, a notable structural change occurred in the sectoral distribution of US outflows. US FDI outflows increased substantially in the tertiary sector – from $3.4 billion in 1983 to a peak level of $27.4 billion in 1989 (Annex 3, Table 9, Chart 3). As a result, the FDI stocks held by this sector increased from 29.2 per cent in 1983 to 48.8 per cent in 1992. The primary industry's share of these stocks decreased from 30.7 per cent in 1983 to only 12.7 per cent in 1992 (Table 7, chart 7).

A driving force behind the rise of the services industry was the finance, insurance, and business services (FIBS) sector. At its peak in 1989, the FIBS sector recorded $22.0 billion, or 58.6 per cent of total FDI outflows in that year (see Annex 3, Table 9, Chart 2). In 1992, this sector's FDI stock was estimated at $159.3 billion, or 32.7 per cent of total US FDI stocks abroad.

Table 7. **Direct investment abroad: position at year-end by industry, 1981-1992**

In US$ million

	1981	1982	1983	% of total	1984	1985	1986	1987	1988	1989	% of total	1990	1991	1992	% of total
PRIMARY	**53 244**	**63 531**	**63 616**	**30.7**	**63 682**	**63 108**	**63 951**	**65 070**	**63 218**	**53 624**	**14.0**	**58 548**	**61 431**	**61 760**	**12.7**
Agriculture	..	504	528	0.3	729	497	378	551	561	582	0.2	581	548	546	0.1
Mining and quarrying	..	5 210	5 514	2.7	4 902	4 916	5 076	4 745	4 850	4 717	1.2	5 155	4 990	6 007	1.2
Oil[1]	53 244	57 817	57 574	27.8	58 051	57 695	58 497	59 774	57 807	48 325	12.7	52 812	55 893	55 207	11.3
SECONDARY	**92 388**	**83 452**	**82 907**	**40.0**	**85 865**	**94 700**	**105 101**	**131 645**	**138 725**	**147 944**	**38.8**	**167 993**	**180 463**	**187 276**	**38.5**
Food, beverages and tobacco[2]	..	7 630	7 661	3.7	8 156	9 252	11 366	12 682	13 281	11 890	3.1	15 331	16 997	18 411	3.8
Textiles, leather and clothing[3]	..	1 395	1 293	0.6	1 169	1 249	1 131	1 453	1 470	1 597	0.4	1 741	1 807	2 209	0.5
Paper, printing and publishing	..	4 700	4 429	2.1	4 930	5 434	5 475	6 436	7 040	10 869	2.8	11 494	12 578	13 652	2.8
Chemical products	..	18 274	18 788	9.1	19 200	20 273	22 653	27 789	31 367	33 563	8.8	37 348	40 712	43 821	9.0
Coal and petroleum products	..	..	..	..	..	..	..	..	..	..	..	..	..	..	..
Non-metallic products	..	3 326	3 224	1.6	3 225	3 546	3 919	5 098	6 076	5 474	1.4	5 720	5 831	5 770	1.2
Metal products	..	5 463	4 974	2.4	5 256	5 012	5 542	6 279	7 939	8 175	2.1	10 474	9 819	10 109	2.1
Mechanical equipment	..	13 840	14 294	6.9	14 816	18 987	22 090	27 766	26 652	26 787	7.0	30 680	31 642	29 174	6.0
Electric and electronic equipment	..	7 292	7 328	3.5	8 193	8 515	7 049	10 055	10 674	13 303	3.5	15 518	16 461	17 001	3.5
Motor vehicles	..	9 922	9 593	4.6	9 754	10 865	12 910	17 619	18 318	20 451	5.4	20 385	22 769	24 529	5.0
Other transport equipment	..	1 046	919	0.4	910	854	1 075	1 133	830	970	0.3	449	1 085	1 051	0.2
Other manufacturing	92 388	10 564	10 404	5.0	10 256	10 713	11 891	15 335	15 078	14 865	3.9	18 853	20 762	21 549	4.4
TERTIARY	**82 716**	**60 769**	**60 680**	**29.3**	**61 933**	**72 442**	**90 748**	**117 592**	**133 950**	**180 215**	**47.2**	**200 419**	**219 060**	**237 634**	**48.8**
Construction	..	1 061	937	0.5	1 069	1 331	1 341	969	1 057	615	0.2	706	796	763	0.2
Wholesale and retail trade	..	24 485	25 184	12.2	24 844	26 787	30 768	36 934	40 430	44 669	11.7	49 952	56 032	59 544	12.2
Transport and storage	..	1 681	1 814	0.9	1 703	1 679	1 542	1 464	1 432	1 811	0.5	2 202	2 445	2 714	0.6
Finance, insurance and business serv.[4]	..	30 526	29 421	14.2	31 102	38 844	53 152	74 050	85 964	125 260	32.8	135 335	145 668	159 335	32.7
Communication	..	116	137	0.1	154	618	660	8	80	371	0.1	2 876	3 603	4 550	0.9
Other services	82 716	2 900	3 187	1.5	3 061	3 183	3 285	4 167	4 987	7 489	2.0	9 348	10 516	10 728	2.2
UNALLOCATED	..	..	..	..	..	..	..	..	..	..	..	..	..	..	..
TOTAL	**228 348**	**207 752**	**207 203**	**100.0**	**211 480**	**230 250**	**259 800**	**314 307**	**335 893**	**381 783**	**100.0**	**426 960**	**460 954**	**486 670**	**100.0**

1. Including petroleum manufacturing products and petroleum related services.
2. Excluding tobacco which appears under "Other manufacturing".
3. Excluding leather which appears under "Other manufacturing".
4. Excluding investment to the Netherlands Antilles.
Source: United States Department of Commerce, Bureau of Economic Analysis: *Survey of Current Business*, various issues.

Chart 7. **Direct investment abroad: position at year-end by industry**

1992

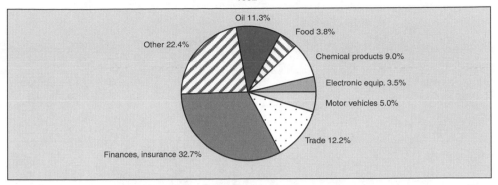

Oil 11.3%
Food 3.8%
Other 22.4%
Chemical products 9.0%
Electronic equip. 3.5%
Motor vehicles 5.0%
Trade 12.2%
Finances, insurance 32.7%

1989

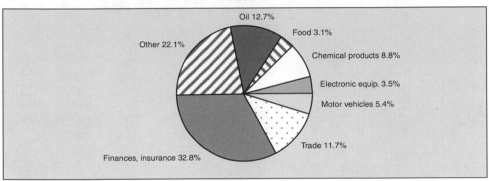

Oil 12.7%
Food 3.1%
Other 22.1%
Chemical products 8.8%
Electronic equip. 3.5%
Motor vehicles 5.4%
Trade 11.7%
Finances, insurance 32.8%

1983

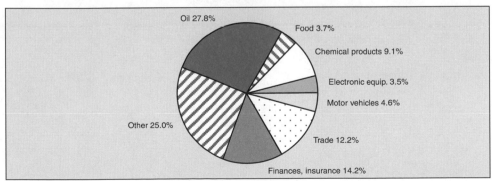

Oil 27.8%
Food 3.7%
Chemical products 9.1%
Electronic equip. 3.5%
Motor vehicles 4.6%
Other 25.0%
Trade 12.2%
Finances, insurance 14.2%

Source: OECD/DAF.

29

Chapter 2

United States policy towards foreign direct investment: recent developments and prospects

A. Overview

FDI policy and practice in the United States are characterised by openness and non-discriminatory treatment of foreign investors, both those already established and those wishing to enter the US market. No general authorisation is required for foreign direct investment in the United States, and foreign investors are accorded fair, equitable and non-discriminatory treatment in most areas of economic activity. Exceptions to the national treatment principle are limited to specific sectors and certain federally-funded technology assistance programmes and USAID contracts and Federal Government air transport contracts.

In a number of sectors, such as atomic energy, air transport, and coastal and domestic shipping, foreign investment limitations have long applied for reasons of national security, but these are commonly found in other OECD countries. Foreign mergers, acquisitions and take-overs of US firms may be notified for national security review. State governments favour FDI and often campaign vigorously to attract it. However, restrictions at state level apply to investments in land, banking, financial services and insurance activities.

In recent years the rise in foreign investment in the United States, and the desire to strengthen US. firms' competitiveness have led to a stronger emphasis on opening foreign markets and to the US government's willingness to consider withholding access to foreign investment in certain sectors to achieve this goal. Pressures have developed in the US Congress and within the Administration for action to monitor or restrict foreign investment. Calls for reciprocity have been especially persistent.

Successive Administrations have worked effectively to reduce or remove some of the most restrictive FDI proposals that have come before the United States Congress. The current Administration strongly opposed an amendment to the National Competitiveness Act of 1993 that would have severely limited foreign participation in some federal technology assistance programmes. The President also stated in his signing statement for the National Cooperative Production Amendments in June 1993, that the Administration would implement the legislation in a way that honours US commitments in treaties and agreements and in various organisations for economic co-operation and development. The President stated in a speech in February 1993 that the US would welcome foreign investment in US businesses but would insist that US investors be equally welcome in other countries.

These efforts notwithstanding, a body of US law has accumulated over the years which is inconsistent with the national treatment and most-favoured-nation principles. Moreover, the United States is no longer attached to a policy of unconditional national treatment in all cases, and concerns have been expressed about the future direction of United States policy in this field.

Foreign investors' treatment in the designation of primary dealers in the financial sector, and in maritime shipping, submarine cable landing rights, air freight forwarding and air charter activities, right-of-way for oil or gas pipelines across on-shore federal lands, and leases to develop mineral resources on on-shore federal lands is conditioned by law on the way US investors are treated in those activities in the foreign investors' home country.

The Administration has, for the first time, unequivocally favoured the passage of conditional national treatment provisions in financial services legislation, and regarded passage of the Fair Trade in Financial Services (FTFS) legislation as a priority matter. The Administration is also considering a proposal to raise the threshold for foreign acquisition of US airlines' voting stock subject to certain conditions, including providing the United States with comparable opportunities, including liberal market access and liberal investment opportunities.

Foreign-controlled enterprises in the United States will not unconditionally receive national treatment under US technology assistance programme such as the 1992 Advanced Technology Programme, the 1993 Technology Reinvestment Project and the 1992 Energy Policy Act. These statutes provide that recipients' participation be in the economic interest of the United States, and that if the

recipient is foreign-owned its parent company's home country provides comparable opportunities for US-owned firms to participate in such programmes. Other
government-supported technology programmes, like the clean car partnership and
the semiconductor technology research consortium (SEMATECH) do not contain
reciprocity or conditional National Treatment provisions; however, there is no
foreign participation because the private partners have not wanted foreign firms.
While no foreign company is included in the clean car partnership, USCAR is
pursuing joint collaborations with its counterpart, EUCAR.

These developments notwithstanding, the United States authorities consider
that their recourse to reciprocity is limited in scope, does not represent any
fundamental change in its FDI policy, and is designed to open foreign markets to
US investors, not protect them from foreign competition. Reciprocity in US
investment law and practice is limited to areas that remain closed to US investors,
or where reciprocity is the rule rather than the exception in international investment relations, as in the financial sector.

Concerns nevertheless remain. Taking into account the importance of the
United States in international investment flows and the leadership role its policy
makers have played in promoting a favourable climate for foreign direct investment, departures from the principles of national treatment and non-discrimination
are naturally regarded with the utmost seriousness, and would be inconsistent
with standstill commitments under the OECD investment instruments.

B. Reciprocity and conditional national treatment

The United States has in the past taken a very strong position of principle
against the use of reciprocity. However, reciprocity measures have been in place
for a number of years in a few sectors. More recently, there have been proposals
introduced in the Congress for new reciprocity measures – or "conditional
national treatment" – in such sectors as banking and securities and air transport,
and Congress has enacted reciprocity measures in technology assistance
programmes.

Under current US law, foreign investors' treatment in air transport-related
activities (*i.e.* freight forwarding, air charter), submarine cable landing rights, oil
and gas pipelines across on-shore federal lands, leases to develop mineral

resources on federal lands, primary dealers in financial services, and maritime shipping is conditioned on the way US investors are treated in those activities in the foreign investors' home country. Most of these provisions are not new. According to the US authorities, no OECD country has failed to meet the reciprocity test in minerals and mining. No primary dealer designation has ever been refused to a foreign applicant on reciprocity grounds.

Conditional national treatment provisions also apply to foreign firms' participation in a number of federally-funded technology programmes. In certain other technology programmes providing assistance to private sector partnerships, foreign firms' participation has not occurred because of membership restrictions by the partnerships themselves. Government technology assistance programmes that apply reciprocal conditions to foreign participation or involve private sector partnerships are discussed in the section on "Promoting US Competitiveness".

It should finally be noted that the United States may take action under section 301 of the Omnibus Trade and Competitiveness Act of 1988 against countries that discriminate against US investors. In March 1994 the President reinstated Super 301 trade law provisions, which require the Administration to identify priority countries and practices from the National Trade Estimate report on foreign trade barriers, which also includes barriers to direct investment.

Recent sector-specific conditional national treatment proposals supported by the US Administration are discussed below, followed by sector-specific conditional national treatment provisions currently in force.

i) Banking and financial services

For a number of years the Congress has been considering legislation that would empower US regulatory authorities to refuse applications for entry and expansion from foreign financial institutions originating from countries not providing effective market access to US financial institutions. While the US Treasury Department initially opposed the adoption of a conditional national treatment requirement in the financial sector, it withdrew its main objections in October 1990 to a version of the legislation that the Senate proposed to include in the long-term Defense Production Act. The 1993 Congress decided to proceed with similar legislation and a bill under the same title and with basically the same provisions – the Fair Trade in Financial Services Act (FTFSA) – was considered by the 103rd Congress but defeated in the House/Senate Conference Committee before reaching the floor of either chamber for a final vote.[6]

As stated in a joint letter by US Trade Representative Michael Kantor and Secretary of Treasury Lloyd Bentsen to Honourable Donald W. Riegle, Jr. Chairman of the Committee on Banking, Housing and Urban Affairs, sent earlier in the year, the passage of this legislation was considered a priority matter and an essential element in the US market opening talks in this field, both within the GATT framework and bilaterally. Indeed, passage of the legislation was regarded by the Administration as being needed quickly to help safeguard the progress achieved in the Uruguay Round and to support scheduled liberalisation negotiations in Geneva during the coming months.

The Administration's support for the legislation was conditional upon a number of considerations that would take account of the unique features of banking and financial services. First, existing operations of foreign financial institutions already established in the United States – including foreign branches – should be fully protected. In other words, the impact of the legislation should be prospective so as not to jeopardise the economic and financial benefits derived from foreign financial institutions already established in the United States. At the same time, the US should not be committed to automatically granting foreign financial institutions – including foreign-controlled institutions already established within the United States – access to new powers, expanded operations in new areas, or new entry that may result from future regulatory developments.

Second, the legislation should provide for ample discretion for negotiators, rather than subject them to automatic mechanisms or rigid deadlines. In seeking market liberalisation, the US Government is looking for substantially full access to foreign markets and national treatment.[7] The United States is prepared to consider, whenever necessary, transitional arrangements with foreign governments that provide time for domestic firms to adjust to greater competition in their home markets.

Third, such legislation should be exercised in a manner consistent with and supportive of US international commitments such as its obligations in the World Trade Organisation to pursue dispute resolution and market access commitments the United States may ultimately make. The legislation should provide the Administration with negotiating leverage in seeking further market access commitments in the financial sector during negotiations that are scheduled to continue until six months after the Uruguay Round Agreement comes into force. The Administration believed that this incentive was particularly needed with respect to countries that maintain a more restrictive regime than the United States.

The US authorities consider that, as most OECD countries have reciprocity provisions in their financial services legislation, the United States was simply following them in attempting to adopt a conditional option in national law in order to encourage foreign countries to open their foreign markets. Moreover, the FTFSA would not have affected countries that have provided the United States with a binding national treatment and a substantially full market access commitment in financial services and that adhered to that commitment in practice.

Concerns nevertheless remained. The FTFSA[8] would potentially have affected established institutions – not just new investors – and its adoption would have added to the existing number of reciprocity measures among OECD Members. The application of a "conditional national treatment" requirement to OECD Member countries would raise questions concerning compliance with the non-discrimination principle of the Codes by the United States, a country which has long played a leading role in promoting unconditional national treatment as the overriding principle in investment policy. It is true that Annex E to the Capital Movements Code provides an exception to the non-discrimination principle, but this annex is limited to reciprocity measures and other forms of discrimination affecting inward direct investment and establishment adopted up to 16 July 1986.

ii) Primary dealers

If a foreign-controlled commercial or investment bank's home government denies national treatment to a US-owned bank to engage in government security operations, the Federal government may refuse to designate that bank as a "primary dealer." Institutions designated as "primary dealers" are required to make markets in government securities and have special borrowing facilities at the Federal Reserve Bank of New York. This law, which has been in force since August 1989, is said to have helped open foreign securities markets to US investors. No primary dealer designation has ever been refused to a foreign applicant on reciprocity grounds.

iii) Air transport

Reciprocity already applies to foreign participation in air freight forwarding and air charter activities in the United States. The United States is considering a proposal to raise the threshold for foreign acquisition of US airlines' voting stock subject to certain conditions. Each of these reciprocity measures – one which is law already and applies to foreign participation in air freight forwarding and air charter activities, and the other which is proposed for foreign acquisition of US airlines' voting shares – are discussed below.

Indirect air transportation: freight forwarding and air charter

US citizens have blanket authority to engage in indirect air transportation activities (air freight forwarding and charter activities other than as actual operators of the aircraft). Non-US citizens must get permission from the Department of Transportation (DOT) to engage in indirect air transportation (air freight forwarding and organising air charters) either by cross-border or establishment for US-originating traffic. (The Department declines to exercise its jurisdiction over foreign-originating indirect air transportation.) Applications for such authority may be denied for reasons of public interest or failure of effective reciprocity. The Department of Transportation determines whether an applicant's country of origin affords like opportunities to US citizens, based on evidence provided by the applicant and/or by inquiry to competent homeland authorities. Interested parties may also comment on the application.

Upon a favourable determination by DOT, indefinite registration is granted to the applicant, and subsequent applications from the same nationality are routinely approved. Foreign domiciled firms applying to provide US-originating indirect air transportation must designate an agent for service of process in the United States.

Until 1981 foreign indirect air carriers were subject to the same licensing procedures as foreign direct air carriers (airlines), and reciprocity was an element of the public interest determination required for such a licence. Simplified registration procedures adopted in 1981 made reciprocity an explicit criterion. Since 1981 there have been no denials of foreign charter operator registrations, of which there are 106 by nationals from 29 countries. Foreign freight forwarder registration has been denied approximately 6 times in the case of firms from four countries; there are 256 registrants from 42 countries.

Foreign purchase of US airlines' voting stock

In January 1994 the Secretary of Transportation announced a plan to revitalise the United States airline industry, in part by raising the limit on the amount of voting stock private foreign investors can hold in US airlines.[9] The Administration is considering a proposal that would raise the limits on foreign voting shares from 25 to 49 per cent if there is an air service agreement with the government of which the investor is a national that would permit expanded investment opportunities for privately-owned and controlled foreign airlines and provide the United States with comparable opportunities, including liberal market access and liberal investment opportunities.

The Administration proposal to raise the limit on the amount of voting stock foreigners can hold in US airlines excludes government-owned airline investors. It is felt that allowing foreign government-owned entities to invest in US airlines could lead to unfair competition with privately-held US carriers. The concern is that government-owned airlines might be guided by political considerations, rather than or in addition to economic considerations. Another concern is that many foreign government-owned airlines receive state aid, and that the availability of such funds to the US carrier that is owned by a foreign government-owned airline could distort competition with its US competitors, whose access to capital is based purely on economic considerations. The proposed legislation will therefore limit the liberalisation to investment by privately-owned investors.

iv)   Minerals mining

Non-US citizens may own 100 per cent interest in a US corporation that acquires a right-of-way for oil or gas pipelines across on-shore federal lands, or that acquires a lease to develop mineral resources on on-shore federal lands, unless the foreign investor's home country denies similar or like privileges for the mineral or access in question to US citizens or corporations, as compared with the privileges it accords its own citizens or corporations or to the citizens or corporations of other countries.

v) *Submarine cable*

In order to assist US citizens in foreign countries to secure cable operation and landing rights, the President may authorise the Federal Communications Commission to withhold or revoke a licence from a foreign firm to land or operate a submarine cable to or from the United States. This authority is provided under the Submarine Cable Landing Licence Act of 1921.

While there have been no denials or revocations of submarine cable landing rights to foreign-owned firms, there have been contested applications and licences granted conditionally. The most recent conditional grant was to a US licensee owned 20 per cent by a Canadian company. In this case the FCC issued a conditional licence for a submarine cable between the United States and Canada. The FCC is withholding a final licence until the Canadian parent company demonstrates that US entities have been provided a reasonable opportunity to participate in the planning and manufacture of the cable system, in which the Canadian firm apparently holds a monopoly position.

vi) *Maritime transport*

Under the Foreign Practices Shipping Act of 1988, the Federal Maritime Commission may take action against foreign carriers if the foreign carrier or its government is a contributing cause to conditions which adversely affect US carriers in US oceanborne trade and which do not exist for foreign carriers of that country in the United States.

The Federal Maritime Commission has initiated action against three countries under the Foreign Shipping Practices Act of 1988: Japan, Taiwan, and the People's Republic of China. Sanctions were never imposed as each of these cases was satisfactorily resolved.

C. Promoting United States competitiveness

i) *Introduction*

The United States does not have what is formally called industrial policy, but for many years the Federal Government has been an active and important provider of funds for basic research and development activities, mostly in military technologies, energy development and agriculture. Throughout the post war period, federal funds have accounted for between 45 and 60 per cent of total national R&D spending.[10] Although federal R&D funding in the United States is smaller as a proportion of GNP than several OECD countries', it is nonetheless very large and figures prominently in the nation's R&D effort.[11] In aircraft, high-performance computers, and agriculture, the federal government had a direct role in the creation of industries that today are globally competitive and generate export surpluses for the United States.[12]

During the 1980s, Congress enacted several laws to indirectly support technology development in the private sector and promote government-industry collaboration. The Administration now wants to increase funding for technology assistance programmes, and has made clear that it will reorient a significant fraction of Federal R&D to help industry develop and profit from innovations.[13] In February 1993, the Administration introduced a technology policy that has several important features and is a key element of the President's National Economic Strategy.[14] Technology policy is seen as important not only to defence but to strengthen the US economy. Over time the United States hopes to devote a larger share of federal R&D to commercial applications rather than military uses. Whereas today only 41 per cent of the federal R&D budget funds civilian research, the Government hopes that by 1998 federal support for civilian or dual use R&D will be more than 50 per cent of the total R&D budget.[15]

The United States appears more willing than in the past to engage in business-government co-operative efforts to meet commercial goals, and is less reluctant to provide government funding and guidance to do so. The automobile partnership between the US government and the ''Big Three'' US auto makers, which will involve government and industry financing to develop a more fuel efficient automobile is one example of this. The proposal to significantly expand funding for the Advanced Technology Programme and the Advanced Research Projects Agency, both of which involve government support for commercially applicable R&D, is another example of the increased emphasis on business-government co-operation.[16] And the 1993 law that gives joint ventures in manufacturing limited anti-trust immunity is still another example of the importance the United States gives to technology policy.

ii) Implications of US technology policy for foreign direct investment

The focus on greater business-government collaboration in technology development and commercialisation has implications for US foreign investment policy. In particular, the question arises as to whether established foreign-controlled enterprises in the United States will receive national treatment under US technology assistance programmes.

Three US government-sponsored technology programmes condition foreign participation on the way US companies are treated in similar programmes in the foreign applicant's home country.

These laws – the American Technology Preeminence Act, the Technology Reinvestment Project and the Energy Policy Act – which were passed in recent years require that **any** recipient's participation in such programmes would be in the economic interest of the United States. But if the recipient is foreign-owned, even if it is established in the United States, it must generally meet an additional test in which its parent company's country of incorporation must provide: *i)* comparable opportunities to US-owned firms to participate in such programmes; *ii)* comparable local investment opportunities to US-owned firms; and *iii)* adequate and effective protection of US intellectual property rights.

Not all US research programmes condition the participation of foreigners, however. The High Performance Computing and Communications Program (HPCC), initiated in 1991 and now part of the National Information Infrastructure Program, has no eligibility criteria for the participation of foreign-owned firms. The HPCC funds research to create more powerful computers, faster computer networks, better software, and to address complex engineering and scientific problems. The United States' major concern is that government R&D be carried out in a manner that promotes US competitiveness and economic growth. The definition of "US company" or "eligible company" in a number of government-sponsored R&D programmes (Advanced Technology Program, Technology Reinvestment Project, National Cooperative Research and Production Act) allows the subsidiaries of foreign-owned firms to participate subject to the goals of the programme, which are intended to ensure that the benefits of the programme accrue to the US economy.

By including reciprocity provisions for a number of federally-supported technology assistance programmes, it appears that the Congress wished to ensure that US-owned companies overseas got similar access to foreign government-sponsored R&D programmes; was concerned by what it considered to be the inadequate market access that US companies faced in various overseas markets and sectors; and was responding to concerns about protection of intellectual property rights.

iii)   National Cooperative Research and Production Act of 1993

The National Cooperative Research and Production Act of 1993 became law on 10 June 1993. This statute amends the 1984 National Cooperative Research Act by extending the more favourable antitrust treatment now given R&D joint ventures to manufacturing joint ventures as well. Its purpose is to encourage the establishment of joint ventures in manufacturing by effectively limiting the application of antitrust laws by limiting damages to single rather than treble in antitrust suits.

One important difference between the 1993 National Cooperative Research and Production Act and the 1984 National Cooperative Research Act is that the 1993 act contains reciprocity conditions and the 1984 act does not: for **any** research and development joint venture covered by the 1984 Act, limited antitrust immunity is granted automatically upon filing the required notification under the Act.

In order to receive the 1993 law's antitrust benefits, the joint venture's principal facilities must be located in the United States. Also, each party (and each person who controls a party) must be a US person or a person from a foreign country that accords antitrust treatment to US persons no less favourable than to its domestic persons with respect to participation in production joint ventures.[17] Foreign firms, therefore, may be eligible for the law's antitrust benefits, but only under reciprocal conditions.

While persons from OECD countries are not excluded from the reciprocity test in the legislation itself, the legislative history clarifies Congressional intent and the President's signing statement says the legislation would be implemented in a way that honours the commitments as set forth in "treaties of friendship, commerce and navigation, bilateral investment treaties, and free trade agreements, and various organisations for economic co-operation and development."[18]

iv) 1993 Defense Appropriations Act and the Technology Reinvestment Project

The 1993 Defense Appropriations Act provides authorisation and funding for the Technology Reinvestment Project (TRP), which is administered by the Defense Department in co-operation with other federal agencies, and was appropriated almost $472 million in 1992.[19] The project provides funding for technology and industrial support programmes on a cost-sharing basis with private businesses and consortiums. To participate in the TRP a company must conduct a significant level of its research, development, engineering, and manufacturing activities in the United States. A firm not meeting this test may still be eligible if its majority ownership or control is by US citizens. In addition, a foreign-owned firm may be eligible if its parent company is incorporated in a country whose government encourages US-owned firms' participation in R&D consortia to which that government provides funding, and affords effective intellectual property rights for US companies. Foreign firms' eligibility in TRP will be determined by the Secretary of Commerce, with the burden of establishing eligibility resting on the proposer.[20]

Projects are chosen on the basis of technical merit, commitment to develop commercial products, and impact on the economy and defense needs. TRP selection has included a number of foreign-owned firms; countries participating in TRP programmes have included Canada, Denmark, France, Japan, Switzerland and the United Kingdom.

v) The Energy Policy Act of 1992

The Energy Policy Act of 1992 (PL 102-486) was signed into law on 24 October 1992. It authorises federal programmes to provide financial assistance and industry-government joint ventures to provide financial assistance to industry for a number energy-related purposes. These may include assistance for research and development in fuel efficiency, renewable energy, and advanced manufacturing in the energy sector. To receive funds under the Energy Policy Act of 1992, a company must show that its participation will be in the economic interests of the United States, as evidenced by investments in the United States in research, development and manufacturing. It must also be a US-owned company or a company incorporated in the United States whose parent is incorporated in a country which: *i)* affords to US-owned companies opportunities comparable to those afforded to any other company to participate in such joint ventures; *ii)* affords US-owned companies local investment opportunities comparable to those afforded any other company; and *iii)* affords adequate and effective intellectual property rights of US-owned firms.

vi) American Technology Pre-eminence (ATP) Act of 1991

This act was signed into law on 14 February 1992, and authorises the Advanced Technology Programme to fund businesses in the research and development of technologies to stimulate high-risk, high-potential products, processes and technologies.[21] The Commerce Department's National Institute of Standards and Technology is the lead agency for developing technology partnerships through the ATP, which started with a budget of around $10 million, then increased to about $200 million in 1994. Congress appropriated $431 million to the ATP for 1995, and the budget plan for 1997 is $750 million.

The primary focus in implementing the ATP has been to promote projects and invest in technology in a way that will have positive benefits to US competitiveness in terms of job creation, economic growth, investments in R&D manufacturing, and a strong supplier base. ATP eligibility is determined under a two-step process. First, a company must show that its participation will be in the economic interest of the United States as evidenced by the following:

   i) investments in the United States in R&D and manufacturing;
   ii) significant contributions to employment in the United States; and
   iii) agreement with respect to any technology arising from assistance provided to promote within the US the manufacture of products resulting from that technology, taking into account the goals of promoting competitiveness of US industry. In this stage the business and R&D plans of the project are assessed and a judgement is made regarding the benefits

to the US economy, the technical merits of the proposal, and the business plan presented. This is a non-discriminatory process under which US and foreign companies are subject to the same criteria. Proposals are scored and ranked by a federal evaluation board, and applicants whose proposals rank highest will be reviewed orally at National Institute of Standards and Technology.

If a proposal is scored high enough during the review to be considered for an award, then foreign-owned companies must meet several additional requirements to qualify for financial assistance under the programme. The Secretary of Commerce must find that the company is incorporated in the United States and has a parent company which is incorporated in a country which:

i) affords to US-owned companies opportunities comparable to those afforded any other company to participate in any joint venture similar to those under the ATP;

ii) affords to US-owned companies local investment opportunities comparable to those afforded to any other company; and

iii) affords adequate and effective protection for US-owned companies' intellectual property rights.[22]

The definition of "US companies" in the ATP programme allows subsidiaries of foreign-owned companies to participate subject to the programme's goals. British and Dutch companies received ATP awards in December 1993 for project proposals that provide significant investments in US R&D and manufacturing and that have substantial market impact potential. The additional eligibility criteria for foreign firms are only applied in the final stages of the application process, once a company is proven to be a strong potential candidate based on its technical and business merits. No foreign company has ever been turned down for an ATP award for any reason other than the non-discriminatory criteria described above.

To make these eligibility determinations for foreign-owned firms, information and advice is sought from various sources, including the United States Trade Representative, the US Department of Commerce's International Trade Administration and other US Government agencies; from science and technology offices, commercial offices and US embassies in the countries in question; science counsellors in the relevant foreign embassies in the US; managers of the foreign counterpart programme to ATP; written programme documents and related reports; and other US data sources.

On the specific question of whether foreign countries afford US-owned companies comparable local investment opportunities, the determination is based on consultations with USTR, expert opinion and other factors. Countries that are considered to impose barriers to direct investment are cited by USTR in its National Trade Estimate (NTE) Report on Foreign Trade Barriers. Interviews with USTR country specialists may determine if a country is either cited or listed for possible future citation in the NTE.

The Advanced Technology Programme conditions foreign participation in two ways: first, by treating foreign-controlled companies in the United States differently from US companies, and second by leaving open the possibility of according National Treatment to investors from some OECD countries but not others. The Technology Reinvestment Project has similar provisions, as does the National Cooperative Research and Production Act, and the Energy Policy Act of 1992. These measures, all of which are listed as exceptions to the OECD National Treatment instrument, are contrary to the NTI standstill understanding agreed by OECD Member countries in 1988 and confirmed in 1991.

vii) Semiconductor Technology Research Corporation (SEMATECH)

The Semiconductor Technology Research Corporation (SEMATECH) was established in 1987 with federal support from the Department of Defense. SEMATECH's goal was to provide US-owned semiconductor companies with the capability to achieve world leadership in semiconductor manufacturing technology by 1993. In addition to its headquarters and major research and production facilities, SEMATECH has established research centres in 11 universities and has joint programmes with two of the US national laboratories. SEMATECH's current focus is to improve the products of semiconductor equipment suppliers and strengthen the links between semiconductor manufacturers and suppliers. The federal government supplies half of the SEMATECH's $180 million annual budget, with the remainder paid for by its eleven members. Membership in SEMATECH is, under its by-laws, restricted to US companies.

The federal law that funded SEMATECH did not have this membership limitation, however, and SEMATECH and JESSI, the European semiconductor consortium, are discussing ways to advance co-operation.

viii) The US business-government automobile partnership

The "Partnership for a New Generation of Vehicles" between the three American automobile makers (USCAR) and the United States government announced in September 1993 has been described by President Clinton as a model for a new partnership between government and industry.[23] This automobile initiative is designed to achieve a number of specific goals, including advanced manufacturing techniques and near-term improvements in automobile efficiency, safety and emissions. The partnership makes available to US industry expertise and funds from the Departments of Defense, Energy, Commerce, Transportation, NASA and other participating agencies. Federal research laboratories will play a major role in the programme, which plans to use advanced technologies developed by the federal weapons labs. The Government and auto industry will assemble a joint team of scientists and engineers to develop a list of research and development projects. Funding will come from government and industry, the respective shares of which will vary from project to project, depending on whether the projects are long or short term. The US authorities have said that there are no provisions in the partnership's "Declaration of Intent" to exclude foreign participation and that there have been no Administration statements, official or unofficial, that imply this to be the case. It is the case, however, that no US automobile company is excluded and no foreign company is included in the partnership.

The private sector and the government are currently engaged in a technical evaluation of the programme's potential components. There is no specific time frame for establishing R&D projects, and according to US authorities nothing can be done until the programme's technical assessment has been completed. In December 1993, the Departments of Commerce and Energy put forward generic procedures for Cooperative Research and Development Agreements (CRADA) that will facilitate the government's quick response to R&D needs to be identified under the initiative. Similar generic procedures have been put forward by the Department of Defense and NASA. These procedures cover R&D conducted in federal laboratories.

D. International initiatives

Multilateralism has traditionally been a linchpin of the United States foreign economic policy, and US commitment to international economic liberalisation is evidenced by its leading role in the GATT and other international economic organisations including OECD. Bilaterally, the United States has been engaged since the early 1980s in negotiating investment treaties, mostly with developing countries and countries from Eastern Europe and the former Soviet Union. Thirty bilateral investment treaties have been negotiated which generally provide for non-discrimination, free transfer of capital and returns, prompt, adequate and effective compensation, international arbitration, and discipline on performance requirements.

In recent years, while continuing its efforts in multilateral fora, the United States has actively pursued liberalisation of foreign investment through bilateral and regional initiatives. In particular, the completion of the North American Free Trade Agreement (NAFTA), the greater profile and clearer mandate of the Asia-Pacific Economic Co-operation forum, and the goals set by the Japan-united States Framework for a New Economic Partnership all signal a US desire to upgrade investment issues internationally, and a willingness to press for open investment policies in other countries using a range of instruments.

NAFTA contains important and innovative provisions for liberalising direct investment. It includes broad liberalisation based on the principles of national treatment and non-discrimination, protection for foreign investors, dispute settlement procedures for both state-to-state and investor-to-state disputes, and in the case of Mexico, extensive liberalisation. While the US emphasis on establishing closer ties with its neighbours is not completely new – the United States and Canada concluded in 1989 the Canada-US Free Trade Agreement – it does indicate that greater priority is being given to regional integration and liberalisation. However, the commitment of the United States under NAFTA involves no new investment barriers or preferential liberalisation, and non-NAFTA investors enjoy most of the benefits of the substantial liberalisation achieved by the agreement as a whole.

The United States' recent activities in the Asia-Pacific Economic Co-operation forum (APEC) represents a vigorous effort to develop closer and more formal economic ties with countries in the Asia-Pacific region. The United States helped establish APEC in 1989, hosted the first APEC leaders' summit in November 1993, and supports expanding APEC's activities as its members become more comfortable with and committed to greater co-operation.[24] The 1993 APEC leaders' summit confirmed "trade and investment liberalisation as the cornerstone of APEC's identity and activity", and agreed that improving investment rules and procedures in a GATT-consistent manner is a central APEC objective.[25] The Ministers established a new committee on trade and investment to: *i)* create a coherent APEC perspective and voice on global trade and investment issues and increase co-operation among members on key issues; and *ii)* pursue opportunities to facilitate a more open environment for investment and develop initiatives to improve the flow of capital within the APEC region.[26]

The Japan-United States Framework for a New Economic Partnership, often called "the framework talks", represents a strong desire to address anew the persistent imbalance in US-Japanese trade and investment relations. This initiative provides for biannual meetings between the Japanese and American heads of state, as well as ongoing consultations or negotiations between the two governments to remove impediments to international trade and investment flows. Work under the framework is divided into ten "baskets" or topic areas, and investment issues are specifically included in one of the first five baskets being discussed, as are government laws, regulations and guidance that impede market access. Topics may include tax policy, deregulation, real estate regulations and mergers and acquisitions. These discussions are chaired at the sub-cabinet level, and progress in each area will be assessed on objective criteria at the biannual Deputy Minister meetings and, in addition, as agreed by each basket's negotiators. Some concern was expressed about the potential implications of these bilateral contacts for the multilateral principle of non-discrimination. The United States authorities gave assurances, however, that their purpose was not to seek preferential treatment for United States investors, but rather to help reduce the obstacles to FDI in Japan and thereby increase market access for investors from all countries.

E.   State Government policies

The Federal Government is responsible for the conduct of foreign economic policy in the United States, and the ability of state and local governments to regulate foreign ownership is limited by the constitutional prohibition on restriction of interstate commerce. In practice, not many economically significant restrictions on FDI can be found at the state level. Those that do exist are mainly limited to real estate, banking and insurance. In addition, most states have anti-takeover laws which allow corporations incorporated in that state to maintain by-laws which deter their being taken over by domestic or foreign investors. A list of states' restrictions is included in Annex 1.

On the whole, state governments are eager to attract private direct investment and are taking on a substantial and expanding role to do this. Most state governments have set up trade and investment promotion offices to try and attract direct investment, both by foreign and American companies. Forty-four of the fifty states have 156 offices in 22 countries to promote trade and investment. Thirty-seven states have offices in Japan alone and most have offices in Europe.[27] Whereas in 1969 only ten states reported spending any resources to attract FDI, thirty-six states now devote economic resources to attracting or retaining investment on a discretionary basis.[28] The value of incentive packages has escalated, too, particularly for high-impact, high visibility projects. It is estimated, for example, that over $300 million in incentives was paid to attract a single automobile plant in 1993,[29] and that incentive packages in the range of $50 million to $70 million are typical for such investments.[30]

The incentives states provide are familiar: tax abatements, exemptions and credits for land, equipment purchases, or training; grants, below-market rate loans, loan guarantees and low-interest bond financing to provide up-front money to help build or modernise a plant; training and employment assistance; and infrastructure, site improvements and land grants. Almost all states are offering investors some combination of these incentives; taken together, they make for a formidable array of benefits.

As the states provide more and more incentives to attract private investment, state governments are trying determine how to maximise public benefit from incentive-supported projects. Incentives offered by state governments are often contingent on the company's agreeing to create and retain jobs, invest a certain amount of capital, and other contingencies. A survey by the National Governor's Association found that 28 states use some means to hold a company accountable for the investment and job creation commitments on which an incentive is based.[31] The techniques for ensuring accountability include penalties, clawbacks, reporting requirements and other means.

State governments also play an important role in setting the economic and regulatory framework that affects direct investment in their territories. States have or share jurisdiction with the federal government over corporate taxes (discussed in the "Taxes" section), training and education programmes, and environmental, employment and other laws and regulations that are essential elements of the investment environment. Indeed, the availability of dependable utilities, sound and extensive transportation facilities and good educational systems are of prime importance in selecting an investment location.

Notwithstanding states' efforts and resources to attract direct investment, individual state laws may work to restrict the establishment of foreign bank branches and agencies in their territory, for example, and at least six states have reciprocity requirements for banking. Most states whose markets are of interest to foreign banks (*e.g.* California, Pennsylvania, Ohio, Massachusetts, Illinois and New York) welcome foreign banks. Federal law provides that a foreign bank may establish a federal branch or agency in any state where it does not already operate a state-licensed branch or agency and where not prohibited by state law. However, some state laws are more restrictive than federal laws, and range from an outright prohibition of establishment of state branches by foreign bank operations (*e.g.* New Jersey) to the granting of licences under limiting conditions (*e.g.* New York, California and Illinois apply special asset, deposit and/or capital requirements to foreign banking corporations for prudential reasons).

Further, Regional Pact Laws[32] can discriminate against foreign banks' US affiliates that wish to acquire banks forming part of a grouping of banks within a region, usually composed of contiguous States (applicable in Alabama, Arkansas, Florida, Georgia, Indiana, Minnesota, Mississippi, North Carolina, Virginia and Wisconsin). These restrictions generally apply to US banks from outside the regional pact as well, so there is no discrimination based on nationality.

In the insurance sector, a number of states (Colorado, Connecticut, Florida, Idaho, Illinois, Indiana, Minnesota, Nebraska, New York, Ohio, Oklahoma, Washington, Wisconsin) have reciprocity requirements that enable state insurance commissioners to retaliate against perceived unfair insurance trade rules in other countries. A few states (Tennessee, North Carolina, North Dakota) will not issue a licence to insurance companies owned or controlled by a foreign government, and half of the states require US branches of non-US firms to maintain

51

"trusteed surplus funds," which are surplus funds in excess of deposits[33] and are required only of non-US firms.

Insofar as land is concerned, a large number of states have limitations on foreign ownership of agricultural land, while other states' restrictions on foreign investment do not distinguish between agricultural and non-agricultural land. The restrictions on agricultural land vary, from near total prohibitions on acquisition by non-resident foreign-controlled entities of agricultural land (Iowa, Minnesota, Missouri, North Dakota), to prohibitions on non-residents acquiring certain specified sizes of agricultural land tracts (Pennsylvania, South Dakota). Some states limit the amount of land that can be held by aliens, or condition it on the aliens becoming US citizens, or on selling the land after a certain specified period of time (Indiana, Kentucky, South Carolina, Wisconsin, Mississippi, Montana, Oregon).

These restrictions notwithstanding, states laws have not generally had the effect of barring foreign investment in financial services, insurance and land, although the current regulatory system for banking, financial services and insurance is complex. The federal government has ongoing communications with all of the state governments on trade and investment issues, most significantly on the Uruguay Round and NAFTA. These communications provide opportunities to review negotiations and discussions in many areas, including US undertakings on investment matters under the OECD instruments.

Chapter 3

General market access measures

A. Public order and national security

The United States protects its national security interests in international trade and investment activities through legislative and administrative measures, and has statutes restricting foreign investment in a number of sectors for this purpose. In domestic and international air services, most domestic maritime transport, radio and television broadcasting, and production and utilisation of nuclear energy, foreign investment is restricted to protect public order and security.

Despite proposals to liberalise foreign direct investment in US airlines, there are still national security concerns in this sector that will be taken into account in the liberalisation proposals. The United States does not rule out the possibility of future liberalisation in other sectors currently restricted for national security reasons, but the liberalisations would have to be consistent with safeguarding national security.

Other investment-related security provisions include the Export Administration Act and Arms Export Control Act, which limit the export of certain technologies and the Department of Defense's Industrial Security Program, which regulates foreign facilities that hold government contracts for classified work. Contracts to develop and operate government-owned land satellites and to market data from the system are limited to "US private sector parties" to protect national security interests.[34] In extreme cases the International Emergency Economic Powers Act could be invoked, in which the President, after declaring a national emergency, could impose economic measures that might restrict foreigners and their activities.[35]

53

The broadest provision governing FDI in national security is section 721 of the Defense Production Act of 1950, commonly called the "Exon-Florio" provision, amended in 1992. Exon Florio gives the President authority to suspend or prohibit proposed foreign investment projects (mergers or take-overs) or divest completed transactions that might threaten national security – if other laws are not adequate and appropriate to protect national security. A description of the Exon-Florio provision is given in Annex 2.

The OECD Members have discussed at length the question of FDI restrictions based on national security considerations, and the Exon-Florio provision has been an important part of this discussion. The OECD Council has welcomed the liberal manner in which Exon-Florio has been applied and encouraged the US authorities to continue their long-standing open policy towards FDI.

A number of concerns still remain about Exon-Florio, however. In particular, the Exon-Florio provision's lack of a definition of "national security", the possibility of ex post divestment, and the lack of a procedure to review decisions have been criticised for creating uncertainty among some foreign investors about Exon Florio's applicability. The US authorities have explained that it would be impossible to provide a strict definition of national security, and that any broad definition would be too general to give any guidance to investors. Moreover, actions which might curtail the President's power to protect national security raise constitutional issues. The US authorities do not feel, therefore, that additional clarification on Exon-Florio's application and scope is needed at this time.

Another concern is that foreign investors might feel compelled to change their proposals to obtain approval of their investments. Although Exon Florio has resulted in the denial of only one of the 890 cases reviewed (of the 890 transactions notified since 1988 as of the end of September 1994, 15 have gone to the investigative phase and one has been prohibited by the President), this may understate the measure's full impact and influence on foreign acquisitions of US companies. For example, a Swiss-Swedish company proposed a manufacturing joint venture with an American company in 1989, and during the CFIUS investigation the company announced its intentions to maintain production and research and development of the joint venture equipment in the United States. This assurance was specifically cited by the White House when it issued a statement that the President would not block the transaction. Senator James Exon, co-author of the provision, has said the "law has encouraged firms to structure transactions in a manner that would not run afoul of Exon-Florio and has, in some cases, deterred foreign acquisition of high technology companies."[36]

The United States has indicated that the Exon Florio provision has no performance requirements, and that foreign firms wishing to acquire US companies under Exon Florio are required only to provide information on their activities. This is an information request only, and only the facts at the time of the acquisition may be used in the inquiry. Moreover, this information gathering has no policy implications, according to the US authorities, and in fact, the vast majority of mergers and acquisitions by foreign-owned companies in the United States take place without Exon Florio.

Questions were raised as to why, according to the 1992 amendments to Exon Florio, transactions involving government-controlled entities are considered more sensitive than those involving private companies. The US authorities have explained that Congress felt that non-market influences were more likely to be present in government-owned entities than in privately-owned ones, although a number of acquisitions by government-owned entities have already been reviewed by the CFIUS and none had been denied.

B. Taxes

The United States has concluded treaties with over 40 countries to avoid double taxation of income. These treaties, which are generally consistent with the OECD Model Convention, reduce the US withholding tax on dividends paid to foreign shareholders, and also reduce the tax on direct investment interest and interest on bank loans. Moreover, they establish thresholds which permit foreign investors to carry on exploratory or preliminary business contacts in the United States without incurring income tax liability, and assure non-discriminatory taxation of businesses owned or operated in the United States by foreign persons. Finally, the income tax treaties grant tax authorities of the two countries the authority to work together to avoid double taxation.

The United States does not engage in discriminatory practices that affect foreign-controlled corporations, and in most cases the same rules apply to foreign and US-controlled companies. For example, transfer pricing regulations under Section 482 of the Internal Revenue Code apply the same rules to both foreign-controlled and US-controlled enterprises. The United States is participating actively in the project to revise the OECD's 1979 Transfer Pricing Report, and its revised Section 482 regulations are consistent with a draft report that was released for public comment on 8 July 1994. The Committees noted this development and also underlined the importance of the implementation of these regulations.

A separate transfer pricing issue is raised by the unitary tax question, which is a method for determining the state tax for a firm that operates in more than one state. Under this system, state governments prorate the total profits of firms operating in their state by taking into account the shares of in-state sales, payroll and assets in the firms' US totals, and taxing the assigned share.

A number of states, such as California, have attempted to extend unitary taxation on a world-wide basis, and legal challenges have been raised against California's method of applying the formula to world-wide income. A "water's edge" approach had been available, but only upon payment of a substantial fee. In October 1993 the Governor of California signed a bill into law that repealed the fee imposed upon a company electing water's edge taxation. It also eliminated the state tax authorities' ability to disregard a water's edge election under certain circumstances.

In a case before the Supreme Court on this issue, the Administration filed a brief supporting the State of California without speaking to the current US position on world-wide unitary taxation. The brief was based on the argument that the law was not unconstitutional **at the time** the tax was imposed, but the Administration did not take a position on unitary taxation in general. In June 1994 the Supreme Court ruled in favour of California that its unitary method of taxation was constitutional. The ramifications of this ruling are being discussed by the OECD Committee on Fiscal Affairs, which is responsible for this and other tax issues concerning the treatment of international investment.

C. Monopolies and concessions

National monopolies are not an important feature of the American economy, and are limited to certain postal services and the Communications Satellite Corporation. Concessions, defined as granting a limited number of licences in a specific sector, include such activities as mining on federal lands, telecommunications and broadcasting. In broadcasting, for example, any transfer of control of an FCC licence must be pre-approved by the FCC, and since foreign ownership of an FCC licence is prohibited, foreign investments in entities owning FCC licences is restricted. These sectors are competitive in the United States and, in most instances, foreign investors are not excluded. These and other federal licensing rules are discussed in the section on Sectoral Measures.

There are, however, monopolies and concessions at state and local levels, in particular with regard to electric and gas utilities. For example, virtually every state regulates the activities of electric and gas utilities that operate within its boundaries, generally through a public utility commission or some similar body. Other public services such as municipal bus transport are also monopolies at the state and local level. These public services are often subject to competitive bidding, however, and foreign companies are not necessarily excluded.

D. Corporate organisation and private practices

In the United States, as in many OECD countries, a number of company statutes and practices, sometimes sanctioned by law, have the effect of impeding direct investment. Most of these measures are not limited to investment by foreigners but apply equally to foreigner and US investors. These measures frequently involve efforts to avoid take-overs.

By 1989 all but ten states (Alaska, California, Iowa, Montana, New Mexico, North Dakota, Rhode Island, Vermont, West Virginia and Wyoming) had enacted ''anti-takeover'' legislation aimed at protecting their corporations from hostile take-overs. A sample of these statutes include:[37]

1. Business combination statutes, which are designed to prohibit an investor from merging with the target firm for a specified period of time, unless the target's board of directors approves the merger before the firm making the offer obtains a specified percentage of the target's stock. These statutes have the effect of restricting hostile take-overs because a merger is often needed to finance the leveraged transaction on which the take-over would depend. By 1993, 30 states had business combination statutes.

2. Poison pill endorsement statutes, which permit corporations to increase capital through a rights issue which typically permit shareholders (other than the acquirer) to buy shares at a highly concessional price, which would dilute the voting power of the acquirer's shares, making the take-over less attractive. As of April 1993, 23 states had statutes that endorsed companies' poison pill anti-takeover devices.
3. Director's duties statutes, which permits directors faced with a hostile offer to consider more than just the price being offered for the company's stock. Corporate directors may consider, for example, the interests of customers, suppliers, creditors, employees, and local communities, and whether those interests would be best served by remaining independent. Twenty-nine states had laws allowing this in 1993.

States' anti-takeover statutes are not directed against foreign investors specifically but against hostile take-overs generally. Information on how foreign investors have been affected by these statutes is not available, but some statutes have been successfully challenged in US courts.

Another practice in the United States, which is prevalent in many OECD countries provides that some shares, though of equivalent nominal value, carry greater voting rights. These shares with plural voting rights would seem to protect certain shareholders (company founders or directors, for instance) against an overthrow of the majority. United States companies have also developed the practice of "self-tendering", *i.e.* the purchase by a company of its own shares (either for cash or through swap arrangements) to prevent hostile take-overs.

United States firms have developed a number of other techniques for warding off hostile take-overs, too. One is the "white knight". The besieged company calls in a friendly firm which launches a competing take-over bid higher than that proposed by the raider. The target company then merges with the friendly firm.

Chapter 4

Sectoral measures

A. Banking and financial services

The US banking and financial services market continues to be a crucial market for foreign financial institutions with international aspirations. Foreign financial institutions have, in fact, succeeded in taking up a significant share of the US banking and financial services sector. Some 700 foreign banks – the majority operating via branches rather than subsidiaries – account for over one fifth ($850 billion) of the total US banking assets and 35 per cent of business loans. It is estimated that they also generate some 300 000 jobs. In addition, approximately 130 foreign-controlled registered broker-dealers and roughly 200 registered foreign investment advisers are established in the United States.

Two of the main characteristics of the US banking market are its geographical segmentation, which limits the expansion of the bank's branching activities across state boundaries, and strict specialisation rules, which restrict banks from directly carrying on certain securities activities, such as underwriting corporate equity shares, and also restrict ownership of or affiliation links with other kinds of financial institutions or industrial companies, in particular insurance companies and securities firms. Under the dual banking system, however, foreign banks have the option to operate under a federal charter or, where permissible, under a state charter. They can also choose their form of operation (subsidiaries, branches, or agencies or representative offices) provided they fulfil the appropriate prudential requirements.

The US has traditionally pursued a policy of national treatment in this field, seeking equality of competitive opportunity between US and non-US financial institutions. This is true for Federal regulations – where the only major case of

59

discrimination is the requirement that a majority of directors of foreign banks' subsidiaries must be US citizens. It is also the general policy at the state level although there are a number of restrictions of a discriminatory nature concerning in particular establishment and expansion of activities.

Prior to the passage of the International Banking Act (IBA) in 1978, foreign bank branches and agencies were exclusively governed by state law. The IBA extended to foreign bank branches and agencies a number of restrictions applied to US banks, but grandfathered the operations of foreign banks already established and offered an option to operate a federally chartered branch or agency. Since December 1992, both state branches and agencies and US banks chartered under state laws are prohibited from engaging in any activity that is not permissible for federal branches unless exempted by federal US banking regulators. The IBA also provides that all foreign banks with branches, agencies and commercial lending companies in the United States, or companies that control such foreign banks, are subject to the Bank Holding Company Act of 1956 (BHCA), and its restrictions on non-banking activities, generally to the same extent as US banks holding companies.

The Bank of Credit and Commerce International (BCCI) scandal generated some debate in recent years about the status and operation of foreign banks. A new restriction on the ability of foreign banks to operate in the United States through branches was introduced by the Federal Deposit Insurance Corporation Improvement Act (FDICA) of 1991. The FDICIA established that foreign bank establishments which accept or maintain deposits of less than $100 000 have to be in the form of a subsidiary unless they are already in the form of Federally-insured branches – this requirement was limited to retail deposit-taking in 1992. The FDICIA also provided for enhanced supervision of foreign banks by the Federal Reserve Board and more stringent reporting requirements. A review was undertaken in 1992 on whether foreign banks should be required to conduct banking operations in the US through subsidiaries rather than through branches. This study concluded that the guiding policy for foreign bank operations should be the principle of investor choice. The Administration and the Federal banking agencies opposed a subsidiary requirement that would be applied either across the board or for purposes of expanded powers.

Over the years, some flexibility has, however, been introduced in the implementation of the legislation governing segmentation between banking and non-banking financial institutions.[38] More recently, in January 1990, for example, some foreign banks as well as some US banks were authorised to establish subsidiaries to engage in underwriting and dealing in corporate debt and equity securities on a similar basis as US-owned bank holding companies (called "section 20 subsidiaries") subject to certain restrictions (also applicable to their US-owned counterparts).[39] Since then other foreign banks have been allowed to establish "section 20 subsidiaries". Exemptions for certain non-banking activities have also been expanded over the years.[40] In addition, the Federal Reserve Board has been willing to exercise greater flexibility with regard the ability of foreign banking groups to maintain their banking and non-banking operations in the United States under certain limited conditions. Amendments introduced in April 1991 in the Federal Reserve Board's Regulation K enable foreign banks to benefit from the QFBO (Qualifying Foreign Banking Organisation) status and therefore to engage in commercial (non-financial) activities in the United States.[41]

The restriction on inter-state branching by banks has also been softened by the Edge Corporation provisions. Both domestic and foreign banks are allowed to set up Edge Act corporations to undertake international banking operations across state boundaries, such as acceptance of deposits by foreign persons or in relation to international or foreign business, or the financing of international or foreign transactions. A number of limitations apply, however.[42]

The US Administration supports the idea of relaxing geographic restrictions on commercial banks in the United States. For the US Treasury, these restrictions have outlived their usefulness and no longer reflect modern bank practice or competition. Their removal could improve the safety and soundness of the banking system as banks would be able to diversify their assets and structure themselves more efficiently. They would be able to compete with non-bank financial providers that face no similar restrictions. Business and consumers would benefit from greater availability of funds, greater competition, greater customer convenience and improved bank performance.

This reform would also bring greater coherence to changes that have already taken place at the state level. While in 1980, over 50 per cent of the states retained highly restrictive intrastate branching policies, 46 states (plus the District of Columbia) currently permit statewide branching. Interstate banking barely existed prior to the Supreme Court decision in 1985 in favour of New England's regional interstate banking regulation. Today, all states but Hawaii allow out-of-state bank holding companies to acquire banks within the state. But these laws vary considerably from state to state and do not provide for a truly national approach to interstate banking.

In contrast to the approach of the ill-fated proposals for banking reform in 1991, however, the new US Administration has been of the view that any legislation to further relax geographic restrictions of the should be kept separate from other issues and be considered on its own merits. This reform should also abide by certain principles such as the promotion of competition of efficiency, safety and soundness, fulfilment of consumer and community needs and respect of state interests.[43] In addition, it must provide foreign banks with the same competitive opportunities as US banks.

The House of Representatives and the Senate passed versions of a bill favouring this regulatory reform. The subsequent House/Senate Conference Committee that considered the Riegle-Neal Interstate Banking and Branching Efficiency Act of 1994 interstate agreed in July 1994 that foreign banks would be permitted to branch interstate to the same extent as US incorporated banking organisations. It was recognised that the legislation will contribute substantially to the efficiency and stability of the US banking system, continued economic growth at home, and fair and efficient consumer access to financial services. The House of Representatives passed the final Bill in August and the Senate passed it in September. The President signed the bill on 29 September 1994.

Concern has been expressed recently over the possible imposition by the Federal Reserve of fees on US branches, agencies and representative offices of foreign banks to cover the cost of their examination pursuant to section 203 of the Foreign Bank Supervision Enhancement Act of 1991 (FBSEA). The US experts confirmed that the Federal Reserve had requested public comments on its proposal to charge examination fees on US branches, agencies and representative offices of foreign banks as it was responsible for the implementation fees before the FBSEA. They also informed the Committees that the Interstate Banking and Branching Efficiency Act of 1994 provides for a three-year moratorium on the imposition of Federal Reserve examination fees on foreign banks.

The Committees welcomed this positive development. They nonetheless urged the US authorities to find a permanent solution consistent with the United States obligations under the Codes of Liberalisation.

B. Air transport

In the United States, air commerce covered by the Federal Aviation Act of 1958, as amended, comprises three categories of services.

1. Direct air transportation: US or foreign air carriers carrying scheduled and/or charter passengers and/or freight and mail. The concept of "cabotage" applies only to direct air transportation.
2. Indirect air transportation: Firms other than direct air carriers providing freight or charter passenger transportation on their own account but on aircraft operated by other, direct air carriers.
3. Non-common carrier operations for compensation or hire, usually called "speciality air services". These include various agricultural, industrial and advertising activities.

Under the 1958 Act, only air carriers that are "citizens of the United States" may operate aircraft in domestic air service (cabotage) and provide international air service as US air carriers. Here, a "citizen of the United States" means:

   i) an individual who is a US citizen;

   ii) a partnership in which each member is a US citizen; or

   iii) a US corporation of which the president and at least two-thirds of the Board of Directors and other managing officers are US citizens, and at least 75 per cent of the voting interest in the corporation is owned or controlled by US citizens.

This statutory requirement has historically been interpreted by the Department of Transportation (DOT) (and the Civil Aeronautics Board before it) to require that an air carrier in fact be under the actual control of US citizens. The DOT makes this determination on a case-by-case basis and has provided guidance as to certain lines of demarcation. For example, total foreign equity investment of up to 49 per cent (with a maximum of 25 per cent being voting stock), by itself, is not construed as indicative of foreign control. The Administration is considering a proposal to raise the limit on the amount of voting stock that foreign investors can hold in US airways, from 25 to 49 per cent, but only under certain reciprocal conditions, which are explained in more detail below.

"Foreign civil aircraft" are required to obtain authority from the DOT to conduct specialty air services in the territory of the United States. "Foreign civil aircraft'' are aircraft of foreign registry or aircraft of US registry that are owned, controlled or operated by persons who are not citizens or permanent residents of the United States. Section 41703 of Title 49 of the United States Code [formerly Section 1108(b) Federal Aviation Act (1958)] requires that the country of the foreign aircraft must allow similar authority for US aircraft. Satisfactory reciprocity is assumed, absent evidence to the contrary.

Non-US citizens must get permission from the DOT to engage in indirect air transportation (air freight forwarding and organising air charters) either by cross-border or establishment for US-originating traffic. (The Department declines to exercise its jurisdiction over foreign-originating indirect air transportation.) Applications for such authority may be denied for reasons of public interest or failure of effective reciprocity. The Department of Transportation determines whether the applicant's homeland affords like opportunities to US citizens, based on evidence provided by the applicant and/or by inquiry to competent homeland authorities. Also, interested parties may comment on the application. Upon a favourable determination by DOT, indefinite registration is granted to the applicant, and subsequent applicants of the same nationality are routinely approved. Foreign domiciled firms applying to provide US-originating indirect air transportation must designate an agent for service of process in the United States.

Acquisitions in the air transport sector by foreign enterprises are currently limited to 25 per cent of the voting shares of an air carrier. The Administration is considering a proposal that would raise the limits on foreign voting shares from 25 to 49 per cent if there is an air service agreement with the government of which the investor is a national that would permit expanded investment opportunities for privately-owned and controlled foreign airlines and provide the United States with comparable opportunities, including liberal market access and liberal investment opportunities. Indeed, the US Transportation Secretary has said that the Presidential Aviation Initiative represents the most comprehensive government aviation strategy since the industry was deregulated by 1978 legislation.[44] In light of the sweeping reform of the aviation sector that was announced by the Transportation Secretary in January 1994, OECD Members have been interested in the possibilities for foreigners to compete in the newly liberalised sector.

Any acquisition involving two or more competing air carriers are subject to US antitrust laws and approval by the Department of Justice. Foreign acquisitions involving US indirect air carriers (air freight forwarding and charter activities other than as actual operators of the aircraft) must be notified to the Department of Transportation. Applications may be denied for reasons of public interest or failure of effective reciprocity.

C. Shipping

i) *Registering US flag vessels*

Non-resident investors wishing to document a vessel as US-flag must establish a US company which is documented under US laws; and meet the corporate management requirements under which the owner of the vessel is either:

- *i)* an individual US citizen;
- *ii)* an association or other entity whose members are US citizens;
- *iii)* a partnership whose general partners are US citizens and where the controlling interest is owned by US citizens; or
- *iv)* a corporation established in the United States whose president or other chief executive officer and chairman of the board are US citizens, and where no more of its directors are non-citizens than a minority of the number necessary to constitute a quorum.

In addition, while non-resident investors may establish subsidiary operations and thus register a vessel under the US flag, certain maritime activities are subject to additional conditions.

The Secretary of Transportation must approve the reflagging or the sale, mortgage, lease, charter, delivery, or any other manner of transfer to a non-US citizen of a US-flag vessel owned by a US citizen, or a vessel the last documentation of which was under the laws of the US. Except in wartime or national emergency, approval by the Secretary is not required for the reflagging or the sale, mortgage, lease, charter, delivery, or any other manner of transfer to a non-US citizen of a vessel that is owned in whole or part by US citizens that is not operated under the US flag, and whose last documentation was not under the US flag. In addition, the Secretary may grant blanket approval of certain transactions. In these circumstances, the Secretary's approval would be required in wartime or national emergency or for the reflagging of the vessel. The rationale for this requirement is to maintain control over the US-flag fleet and the US-owned foreign-flag fleet for national security purposes. These restrictions ensure that critical assets are not transferred out of US control without an analysis of the impact of such a transfer. And in maritime cabotage the rationale for the restriction is to maintain a pool of trained seamen and vessels available to be called upon in wartime or national emergency.

ii)   Coastal and inland waterway transportation

In order to engage in coastal and inland waterway transportation of freight or passengers, a vessel must be: *i)* built in the United States; *ii)* documented under US law; and *iii)* owned continuously by ''US citizens.'' For these purposes, a US corporation may qualify as a ''US citizen'' only if 75 per cent of stock or voting interests are owned and controlled by US citizens. However, there are limited exceptions to this rule, *e.g.*, for shipping incidental to the principal business of a qualified foreign-controlled US manufacturing or mining company. Generally, US citizenship requirements do not apply if: *i)* the foreign-controlled US company is registered in the US; *ii)* has its principal place of business in the United States; *iii)* is engaged in mining or manufacturing and; *iv)* the transportation of cargo between points in US waters is incidental to the corporation's operations. The foreign-controlled US company may only transport its own cargo and not the cargo of third parties.

The US citizen ownership restrictions apply to towing and salvaging operations and to dredging and the transport of dredge spoils in the coastal trade. Federal statutes also stipulate that a non-US citizen corporation may not engage in transporting supplies from a point within the United States to an offshore rig or platform on the continental shelf. The restriction on foreign investment in dredging and salvage is to maintain domestic capability for use in wartime or national emergency.

iii)   Preferential cargo

A percentage of export of products supported by US government financing is generally restricted to carriage by US-flag vessels. For Commodity Credit

Corporation agricultural exports, 75 per cent of gross tonnage must be shipped on US-flag commercial vessels. With respect to Eximbank-financed exports, 100 per cent of gross tonnage must be shipped on US flag commercial vessels; however, up to 50 per cent of this requirement may be waived for carriage on a recipient country's flag vessels. Transport of military supplies and personnel effects of military and civilian employees is reserved to national flag. Owners of vessels carrying preference cargo must meet the US flag documentation citizenship requirement, and the vessel must be US-built or under the US flag for three years. There is no foreign control test and the US corporation holding title may be a hundred per cent owned by a foreign corporation.

iv) Foreign Shipping Practices Act of 1988

The Federal Maritime Commission is authorised by the Foreign Shipping Practices Act of 1988; Section 19 of the Merchant Marine Act, 1920 and section 13(b)(5) of the Shipping Act of 1984 to take unilateral action when a foreign government, foreign carrier, or other persons providing maritime-related services engages in activity that adversely affects US carriers in the oceanborne trade; creates conditions unfavourable to shipping in the foreign trade; or unduly impairs access by US-flag vessels to trade between foreign ports. Sanctions proposed under these statutes most frequently affect the cross-border provision of services; however, sanctions could also affect foreign-owned investment in the US (*i.e.* revocation of freight forwarders' licenses, suspension of preferential terminal leases).

v) Hazardous waste incinerator ship

Federal regulations stipulate that a foreign or foreign-controlled enterprise may not operate a hazardous waste incinerator ship. However, in view of the fact that measures relating to the disposition of hazardous wastes mostly involve cabotage operations similar to dredging and salvaging, and no investors applied for licences to operate hazardous waste incinerator ships, these measures were considered during the 1987-1988 examination to fall within the existing US reservation.

vi) *Other shipping restrictions*

There are also restrictions on foreign-controlled enterprises from:

i) obtaining tax deferment benefits for the financing or re-financing of the cost of purchasing, constructing or reconstructing, or operating commercial vessels or gear, or obtaining war risk insurance;

ii) selling obsolete vessels to the Secretary of Transportation;

iii) holding a preferred ship mortgage unless approved by the Secretary of Transportation; and

iv) obtaining construction-differential or operating differential subsidies for vessel construction, reconstruction or operation.

The restriction on purchase of vessels converted by the government for commercial use or surplus war-built vessels sold at special statutory sales price has been repealed. This item will therefore be deleted from current transparency measures regarding maritime subsidies.

D. Deep water ports

Foreign investors must establish a US subsidiary under the US laws and corporate management requirements similar to those for vessel documentation to obtain a licence to own, construct or operate a deep water port (outside the US territorial waters). These requirements apply if a deep water port can be utilised, inter alia, to load and unload commodities or materials (other than oil) transported to and from the United States. Also rigs, platforms, vehicles or structures, which are used for activities pursuant to the Outer Continental Shelf Lands Acts and are built or rebuilt later than one year after enactment of the Acts, must be documented under the US laws.

E. Communications

Current US law and practice governing foreign direct investment in the communications sector is summarised below. However, there may be a change in law as the US Government announced in January 1994 that it would soon present a legislative package to eventually remove legal restrictions on all types of communications companies, including cable, telephone, television and satellite.[45] The plan would permit local telephone, cable and long distance companies to enter each other's markets by eliminating the legal and regulatory barriers that currently restrict the types of business they can do. Instead of local, state and federal regulations for these separate industries, the plan is to have a uniform, new set of regulations to govern all telecommunications activities.[46] The Federal Communications Commission would adopt guidelines for regulation under the new section of telecommunications law. The new telecommunications policy is designed to encourage development of a National Information Infrastructure, a web of communications networks, computers and data bases to be made available across the country.

It is unclear at this point what effect the new communications policy could have on foreign direct investment in the communications sector, but the regulatory and administrative changes that are anticipated are certainly important in setting the economic framework for investment in this important sector. Existing rules affecting foreign investment are set out below.

i) Broadcast, common carrier, and aeronautical radio stations

Under the 1934 Act, foreign governments and their representatives are prohibited from holding radio station licences for wireless communications.

Aliens, foreign corporations or any corporation of which any officer or director is an alien may not hold broadcasting, common carrier or aeronautical radio licences. Moreover, aliens, foreign corporations or foreign governments may not own or vote more than 20 per cent of the stock of US corporations holding radio licences for such services.

In addition, the 1934 Act permits the Federal Communications Commission (FCC), acting in the public interest, to deny or revoke a radio licence for broadcast, common carrier, or aeronautical services to a corporation controlled by another corporation of which any officer or more than 25 per cent of the directors are aliens, or where more than 25 per cent of the stock is owned or voted by aliens, foreign corporations or foreign governments. In practice, corporations proposing to exceed these benchmarks apply to the FCC for a ruling that the investment is in the public interest.

It should be noted that the 1934 Act's statutory provisions do not limit ownership in non-radio-based telecommunications systems or equipment, and foreign-owned companies actively participate in these markets. In addition, the above limits are inapplicable to radio-based operations that do not involve broadcasting (radio and TV), common carrier or aeronautical services, such as cable TV radio links and separate satellite systems.

ii) *Communication Satellite Corporation (COMSAT)*

The Communication Satellite Act of 1962, as amended, applies the 1934 Act's foreign ownership provisions to ownership interests in the Communications Satellite Corporation (COMSAT).

iii) *Submarine cable*

The Federal Communications Commission (FCC), under delegated authority from the President of the United States with concurrence of the State Department, is authorised to issue licences to land or operate in the United States any submarine cable directly or indirectly connecting the United States with any foreign country. Under the Submarine Cable Landing Licence Act of 1921, the FCC may withhold or revoke licences if such action will assist, inter alia, in securing cable landing rights for US citizens in foreign countries. This issue is reviewed in chapter 2, section B *v*).

iv) *Landsat systems*

Under the Land Remote Sensing Commercialisation Act of 1984 (Landsat Act), restrictions or limitations are imposed on foreign investors' operation of remote sensing space systems in the US or in co-operation with US entities. Under the Landsat Act, any contract to operate and sell data from the US Government-owned civil land remote sensing satellite system (Landsats 1-5), or to provide a follow-on system, must be with a "US Private Sector Party", which is defined by the Secretary of Commerce. The contractor must be organised under the laws of the United States, and must meet criteria designed to meet any threats to the national security. These criteria take into account the citizenship of key personnel, location of assets, foreign ownership, control, and influence, and other such factors. As was pointed out in the 1987-1988 examination, however, licences are granted to companies investing in privately owned **land** remote sensing satellite systems under the same conditions, irrespective of their nationality or site of corporation.

This restriction is based on national security because classified information is sometimes transmitted over the Landsat system, and the system has hardware that may not be available to the private sector.

F. Mining

Under the Mineral Lands Leasing Act of 1920, aliens and foreign corporations may not acquire rights-of-way for oil or gas pipelines, or pipelines carrying products refined from oil and gas, across on-shore federal lands, or acquire leases or interests in certain minerals, such as coal or oil. Non-US citizens, however, may own a hundred per cent interest in a US corporation that acquires a right-of-way for oil or gas pipelines across onshore federal lands, or that acquires a lease to develop mineral resources on on-shore federal lands, unless the foreign investor's home country denies similar or like privileges for mineral or access in question to US citizens or corporations, as compared with the privileges it accords to its own citizens or corporations or to the citizens or corporations of other countries. Note that nationalisation is not considered to be denial of similar or like privileges.

While foreigners investing through a US branch office may not obtain licences to mine minerals from the outer continental shelf or deep seabed, they may qualify for such licences through a US subsidiary and by complying with certain corporate management requirements.

G. Energy

i) Ocean thermal energy

Foreign citizens may not obtain licences to construct an ocean thermal energy conversion (OTEC) facility located in the territorial sea of the United States, or obtain a licence to operate a moving OTEC plant ship. A foreign-owned US corporation may, however, obtain a licence if it meets the same corporate management requirements as those needed for the documentation of vessels. (For the definition of foreign-owned corporation, see the section of Communications.)

ii) Hydroelectric power, geothermal steam and associated resources

The United States government maintains restrictions of foreign direct investment in this sector at the both federal and state levels (states measures are summarised in Annex 1). According to the Federal Power Act, only US citizens or US corporations can hold hydroelectric plants licences which are issued by the Federal Power Commission. However, a foreign-owned or controlled enterprise may be granted a licence if the enterprise establishes itself in the form of a US incorporated subsidiary. A similar restriction applies to leases for the development of geothermal steam and associated resources.

The Federal Energy Regulatory Commission (FERC) is authorised to grant licences to any corporation organised under the laws of the United States for the purpose of construction or other public works in the hydroelectric sector. However, the FERC may refuse to issue a licence to a foreign-owned or controlled enterprise located in the United States on public interest grounds. The public interest standard is very broad and may include such issues as the applicant's business experience, financial soundness and technical expertise, as well as the environmental effects of the proposed project. The identity of the investor is but one of the many factors taken into account in the licensing process.

iii) Atomic energy

The federal government maintains restrictions of foreign direct investment in this sector under the Atomic Energy Act of 1954. A licence is required for any person in the United States to transfer, manufacture, produce, use or import any facilities that produce or use nuclear materials. Such a licence may not be issued to any entity known or believed to be owned, controlled or dominated by an alien, a foreign corporation or a foreign government. The issuance of a licence is also prohibited for utilisation of production facilities for such uses as medical therapy or research and development activities to any corporation or other entity owned, controlled or dominated by one of the foreign persons described above. Determinations of foreign ownership or control are made on a case-by-case basis. The reasons behind the restrictions are similar to those for other forms of atomic energy facilities – for example, diversion of nuclear materials, preservation of classified information.

H.   Fishing

At the federal level, fishing and fish processing in the US Exclusive Economic Zone and within the boundaries of any State is generally limited to US flag vessels. United States citizens must own a 75 per cent interest in any corporation owning US flag vessels (larger than 5 net tons) which can engage in fishing, fish processing and fish tendering within territorial waters. To qualify for the US flag, vessels must have been built in the United States and must be owned by a US corporation which satisfies the citizenship requirements which are referred to above in the section on coastal and inland waterway transportation. However, fishing vessels documented before 28 July 1987 may be owned by a foreign-owned US corporation provided that a majority of the board of directors and the chief executive officer are US citizens. These "grandfathered" vessels may be sold to foreign owners who meet citizenship requirements.

Foreign controlled enterprises may not engage in certain fishing operations involving coastwise trade, and foreigners may not hold more than a minority of shares comprising ownership in companies owning vessels which operate in US fisheries. Also, corporate organisation requirements pertain to the registration of flag vessels for fishing in the US Exclusive Economic Zone.

In addition, foreign-flag vessels may not fish or process fish in the 200 natural mile US Exclusive Economic Zone except under the terms of a Governing International Fisheries Agreement (GIFA), or other agreement consistent with the US law. This regulation is subject to Magnuson Fishery Conservation and Management Act.

The United States has introduced restrictions in the fishing sector under the Anti-Reflagging Act of 1987 because of concerns about shell corporations being formed in order to fish in the US Exclusive Economic Zone.

Chapter 5

Conclusions

The United States is the largest recipient and source of foreign direct investment in the world. Its large, robust and dynamic market and long-standing commitment to an open and non-discriminatory investment regime in most areas of economic activity have clearly contributed to its large volume of FDI stocks and flows. The strong surge of FDI inflows from the early 1980's led to a reversal of its traditional position as net exporter of equity capital to one of net recipient. This situation lasted until the early 1990s when FDI outflows again overtook FDI inflows. Inward direct investment has also strengthened again in the last year.

For many years, the United States has played a leadership role in promoting liberal, non-discriminatory treatment of foreign investors. Policy statements by presidents from each of the two major parties in 1977, 1983 and the latest, by President Bush in 1991, have all made clear the US commitment to these principles. Successive Administrations have worked effectively to reduce or remove some of the most restrictive FDI proposals that have come before the United States Congress.

Although the basic commitment to an open investment regime has not diminished, specific measures, programmes and proposals in recent years have created some uncertainty for foreign investors. To the extent they are translated into laws, some of these measures could imply a change in the priorities and approach toward FDI policy in the United States. The US Government has become more concerned with promoting equal competitive opportunity for US firms, and is seeking to open foreign markets to US investors to help achieve this objective. In order to open foreign markets, the United States is now willing in certain cases to link its treatment of foreign investors in the United States with the way its investors are treated abroad. This is designed as an encouragement for more restrictive countries to liberalise, but runs the risk of targeted closing of the US. market to investors from countries that do not respond as the United States would wish. For the same reason, in bilateral, regional and international negotiations, the Administration has made clear that in trying to open foreign markets to US investors it will not always rely on the principles of most-favoured-nation and unconditional national treatment.

For the most part, no legislative action has been taken. However, the current Administration has given its support to proposals that foreign participation in certain sectors, like banking and financial services and air transport, be linked to the treatment of United States firms in these activities abroad. There are also long-standing reciprocity provisions in air charter and freight forwarding activities, mineral leasing rights on federal lands and primary dealers. These provisions have elicited concerns with respect to the United States' traditional emphasis on unconditional national treatment as the overriding principle in investment policy.

The focus on greater business-government co-operation to improve the United States' competitiveness also has implications for foreign investors, and in particular, whether and how they will be able to participate in federally-funded technology programmes. Foreign firms' treatment in a number of these programmes is already linked under US law and practice to the way American firms are treated in similar programmes abroad, and the US government contributes financially to co-operation projects between US firms in which foreign participation has not been allowed.

Regulations governing foreign mergers, acquisitions or take-overs that threaten to impair national security are also important in setting the investment environment in the United States. The ''Exon-Florio'' provision, whose final implementing regulations were published in late 1991, gives the President authority to suspend or prohibit proposed foreign investment projects (mergers or acquisitions) or divest completed transactions that could threaten national security. Exon-Florio's lack of a clear definition of ''national security'', the possibility of ex post divestment, and the lack of a procedure to review decisions have been criticised for creating uncertainty among some foreign investors about Exon-Florio's applicability. Amendments in 1992 assure particular scrutiny of proposed acquisitions by foreign government-owned companies that could affect national security, and also add a transaction's potential effect on US technological leadership in national security areas as one of the factors to be considered. Nevertheless, of the 890 (as of the end of September 1994) transactions notified since 1988, only 15 have gone to the investigation phase and only one transaction has been formally prevented.

State Governments in the United States generally pursue a liberal policy towards foreign investors. In fact, it is not unusual for states to compete to attract FDI by offering generous incentives and other inducements. However, restrictions at state level do exist in some sectors where state regulation plays a major role, as in banking and financial services, insurance and land, all of which are important sectors for international investors.

Finally, the United States has become more engaged in recent years in bilateral and regional initiatives that have implications for foreign investors. It has concluded about thirty bilateral investment treaties and is negotiating others. The North American Free Trade Agreement, the Asia-Pacific Economic Co-operation forum and the Japan-United States Framework for a New Economic Partnership signal a more diversified approach to US external investment relations. While concerns have been raised about the possible implications of this more diversified approach for the multilateral system and the principle of non-discrimination, the results to date have had an overall positive and mutually supportive impact on international investment liberalisation.

The policy of the United States still rests on the view that its interests are best served by a liberal global investment regime. This is evidenced most recently by its support for a binding, new investment agreement in the OECD that would have high standards of liberalisation and investment protection and an effective dispute settlement mechanism. A new phase of intensified work is now underway to produce a framework for an agreement by June 1995.

Notes

1. For a summary of policy issues discussed in the 1970s, see C. Fred Bergsten, Thames Horst, and Theodore H. Moran, *American Multinationals and American Interests*, Washington, D.C.: Brookings Institution, 1978.

2. See, in particular, US Department of Commerce, *Foreign Direct Investment in the United States: An Update*, June 1993 and Edward M. Graham and Paul Krugman, *Foreign Direct Investment in the United States*, 1991.

3. For empirical analysis, see Anderson, G.H., "Three common misperceptions about foreign direct investment", *Federal Reserve Bank of Cleveland*, July 1988; Salvatore, D., "Trade protection and foreign direct investment in the United States", *The Annals of the American Academy of Political and Social Sciences*, April 1991; and Yoshida, M., "Micro-macro analysis of Japanese manufacturing investments in the United States", *Management International Review*, April 1987. A theoretical analysis of FDI emphasising the aspect of the barriers to entry was made by Bhagwati, J.N., E. Dinopoulos, and K. Wang, "Quid pro quo foreign direct investment", *American Economic Review*, May 1992.

4. See Graham, E.M. and P.R. Krugman (1992), and Horstmann, I.J. and J.R. Markusen, "Firm-specific assets and the gains from direct foreign investment", *Economica*, February 1989.

5. See in particular John H. Dunning, *American Investment in British Manufacturing Industry*, London: George Allen & Unwin; Stephen H. Hymer, *The International Operations of National Firms*, Cambridge, MA: MIT Press, 1976; Charles P. Kindleberger, *American Business Abroad: Six lectures on Foreign Direct Investment*, New Haven, CT: Yale University Press, 1969.

6. The discussion over reciprocity began in 1987 when the US Senate passed a bill entitled "National Treatment of Financial Institutions" which proposed a policy based on conditional national treatment. The bill was not approved by the House. In 1988, the Senate approved a conditional national treatment requirement for banks and securities firms as part of the Financial Modernisation Act but the House did not concur. The "Fair Trade in Financial Services Act" was introduced, for the first time, to the US Senate in January 1990 by the Chairman of the Senate Banking Committee, Senator Donald W. Riegle Jr., and its ranking minority member, Senator Jake Garn. A revised version was approved and included in the 1990 Defense Production Act Amendments but Congress adjourned without adopting these provisions. The Riegle-Garn legislation was again reintroduced by Senators Riegle and Garn in 1991 as part of the short-term Defense Production Act (DPA), the long-term DPA and the Comprehensive Deposit Insurance Reform and Taxpayer Protection of 1991 ("banking bill"). In the summer of 1991, Congressman Charles E. Schumer introduced a version of the legislation in the House of Representatives that was similar in many respects to the Senate version of the legislation. FTFS was dropped from the short-term DPA and the banking bill, both of which were signed into law. Senator Riegle agreed to drop the legislation from the banking bill with the proviso

79

that the issue be addressed as part of the long-term DPA in the second session of the 102nd Congress. In response to the Senate, a House Banking Subcommittee in March 1992 marked up Congressman Schumer's version of the legislation for inclusion in the long-term DPA. In May 1992, the House Ways and Means and the Energy and Commerce Committees introduced their own version of the legislation. No compromise was reached in 1992. In October 1993, a Fair Trade in Financial Services bill was introduced simultaneously in the House and the Senate. The Senate passed a Fair Trade bill on 17 March that became Title V of the Community Development Banking and Financial Institutions (CDFI) bill. There was no consensus version passed by the House. The House/Senate Conference on CDFI, including Fair Trade in Financial Services, did not adopt FTFSA.

7. The bill set out a five stage process to achieve this objective. As a first step, the Secretary of the Treasury would have been required to identify countries that deny national treatment to US financial institutions. As a second step, the Secretary would have determined whether such a denial had a significant adverse effect on their activities in the foreign country concerned. The main factors to be taken into account for banking organisations would have been: the size of the foreign country's market for banks and the financial services concerned and the extent to which US banking organisations operate and wish to operate these markets; the extent these organisations may participate in the development of new regulations, guidelines and policies; the extent to which these regulations are based on objective standards and are transparent; the extent to which US organisations may offer foreign exchanges services in the foreign country; and the effects of the regulatory policies of the foreign country on capital requirements, regulation of deposit interest rates, restrictions on the operations and establishment of branches and restrictions on access to automated teller machine networks in the country. Third, the Secretary would initiate negotiations with the government of that country with a view to eliminating the denial of national treatment. Fourth, should the negotiations fail to obtain a satisfactory commitment to market access and national treatment in banking and securities, the Secretary of Treasury would have been entitled to publish the determination of a significant adverse effect on US firms. Only after publication would the Secretary have been permitted to recommend to the appropriate federal regulator that it deny any application for entry into the US financial sector. The March 17 Senate-passed version of FTFSA also would have established a parallel set of procedures, negotiating authority and sanctions for the insurance sector. For instance, if a state insurance commissioner did not act within 90 days on a recommendation, the President would have been entitled to impose sanctions.

8. The Senate passed-bill on 17 March 1994 would have permitted, but not required, the Executive Branch to apply a conditional market access and national treatment requirement for the approval of applications from foreign banking and securities firms to acquire facilities or engage in activities at a new geographic location or engage in new activities or expand existing operations. Existing activities of existing banking and securities institutions would have been grandfathered. The requirement for consultation with in the Executive branch would have been strengthened and the flexibility and discretion provided for decision making would have been preserved. In addition, the independence of the federal regulatory agencies would have been affirmed by providing them explicit authority to reject a recommendation to impose sanctions if the safety and soundness of the financial system or investor protection were likely to be impaired.

The final Senate-passed bill also contained two noteworthy changes compared with the original October 1993 version. First, insurance would have been included in the scope of the legislation. Second, the scope of potential sanctions in the securities area would have been expanded in order to equalise the treatment of the securities industry, which is subject to a greater degree of federal regulation in the United States.

9. "Administration Announces Plan for Aviation Industry", *Notes on Economic Affairs*, 7 January 1994, United States Information Service.

10. *The Government's Role in Civilian Technology: Building a New Alliance*, National Academy of Sciences, National Academy of Engineering, Institute of Medicine, National Academy Press, Washington, D.C., 1992.

11. The federal research programme includes more than 700 federal laboratories, hundreds of university research facilities, 2.5 million scientists and engineers, and a national research budget of $76 billion. See "Don't Tread on My Lab", *Time,* 24 January 1994. See also "Whither US Industrial Policy?" Edward M. Graham, in *International Industrial Policy*, Westview Press, edited by Gavin Boyd.

12. See note 11.

13. "A Strategy for American Competitiveness in a New Economic Era", Address before the First Annual Symposium on "Coupling Technology to National Need", by Dr. Mary Good, Under Secretary for Technology, US Department of Commerce, 26 August 1993.

14. "International Trade and Technology Policies", Statement by Laura D'Andrea Tyson, Chair, President's Council of Economic Advisers, before House Committee on Science, Space and Technology, Subcommittee on Technology, Environment and Aviation, 22 March 1993.

15. See note 14.

16. "Commerce ACTS: Advanced Civilian Technology Strategy", US Department of Commerce, November 1993. Also from interviews with Department of Commerce officials, 6 January 1994, and in "Brown Boosts Budget for Commerce Department by Appealing to Clinton's Investment Agenda", *Wall Street Journal*, 5 January 1994.

17. "National Cooperative Production Amendments of 1993", P.L. 103-42, section 4306.

18. Weekly Compilation of Presidential Documents, 14 June 1993. p. 1058, Washington, D.C.

19. "American Technology Pre-eminence Act", P.L. 102-45, section 13525.

20. See note 19.

21. Section 5131 of the 1988 Omnibus Trade and Competitiveness Act authorised ATP. See *The Government Role in Civilian Technology*, National Academy of Sciences, National Academy of Engineering, and Institute of Medicine, National Academy Press, Washington, D.C., 1992.

22. See note 19.

23. White House fact sheet, "A New Partnership for Cars of the Future", 29 September 1993, and "Clinton Announces New Partnership to Build Cars of Future", *Notes on Economic Affairs*, US Information Service, 7 October 1993.

24. Charlene Barshefsky, Deputy US, trade representative, cited in the *Financial Times*, 15 November 1993.

25. APEC Ministers' Joint Statement on Ministerial Meeting, Asia-Pacific Economic Co-operation Ministerial Meeting, 17-19 November 1993, Seattle, Washington.

26. According to the APEC Ministers' Statement: "The objectives of the APEC Committee on Trade and Investment are not limited to investment liberalisation but include developing initiatives to improve the flow of goods, services, capital and technology, consulting on issues, etc." See Annex 1, paragraph 2 of the APEC Ministers' Joint Statement on Ministerial Meeting, Asia-Pacific Economic Co-operation Ministerial Meeting, 17-19 November 1993, Seattle, Washington.

27. "Going Global: A Governor's Guide to International Trade", National Governor's Association, Washington, D.C., 1992.

28. "Investing in America's Economic Future: States and Industrial Incentives", National Governor's Association, Washington, D.C., 1992.

29. "States' Bidding War over Mercedes Plant Made for Costly Chase", *Wall Street Journal*, 25 November 1993.

30. *The New Competitors*, Norman Glickman and Douglas Woodward, Basic Books, Inc., New York, 1989.

31. See note 28.

32. "Regional compacts" allow banks from a specified group of states to set up banking subsidiaries or acquire banks in those states, but exclude banks not included in the region.

33. *National Treatment for Foreign-Controlled Enterprises*, OECD Paris, 1993.

34. United States response to OECE questionnaire on the application of measures and practices relating to public order and essential national security interests as they concern foreign direct investment, March 1993.

35. "US Investment Policy and Exon-Florio", Steven J. Canner, Staff Chairman of the Committee on Foreign Investment in the United States, 25 July 1989.

36. *Oversight of Exon-Florio Amendment: Hearing before the Senate Committee on Commerce, Science and Transportation*, 102 Congress, 1st session. In "The Final Exon-Florio Regulations on Foreign Direct Investment: The Final Word or Prelude to Tighter Controls?" Alan F. Holmer, Judith H. Bello, Jeremy O. Preiss, *Law and Policy in International Business*, Vol. 23, 1992. p. 611.

37. "Mergers and Acquisitions in the United States", Winthrop, Stimson, Putnam and Roberts, May 1993.

38. The separation between banking and securities activities was established on the eve of the Great Depression, with the adoption of the Glass-Steagall Act in 1933, which places strict limits on banks' own securities activities and provides that banks may not be affiliated with firms engaged principally in securities underwriting and dealing activities. The Garn-St German Act of 1982 restricted permissible insurance activities of bank holding companies. These laws also apply, by virtue of the BHCA, to foreign banks and companies that control a foreign bank organised under the laws of foreign countries, if the bank has branches, agencies or commercial lending company subsidiaries in the United States. However, the statutes and regulations provide certain exceptions in recognition of the differing structures of financial systems in foreign countries.

39. In particular, total revenue of such subsidiaries could not exceed 10 per cent of the total revenue of the banking organisation and a number of funding, interlocking and other dealing restrictions were imposed between the security subsidiary and the banks in the same group.

40. For instance, banks have been allowed to underwrite and deal in different kinds of government securities, to engage in future transactions in financial instruments, to securitise and sell their own assets, and to act as agent in the private placement of debt and equity. Banks have also been allowed to engage in insurance brokerage and underwriting for certain kinds of insurance policies.

41. The revised Regulation K also provides that non-qualifying foreign banks or banking organisations could be granted case-by-case exemptions to be able to maintain both their banking and non-banking activities in the United States.

42. Edge corporations must comply with certain capitalisation requirements. They may not take deposits from domestic sources which are not specifically related to international transactions.

Edge Corporations are regulated by general lending and acceptance limits and subject to the reserve requirements that apply to member banks of the Federal Reserve System.

43. While the Administration supports consolidation of banking subsidiaries, it was reluctant to support the idea of introducing market share limits and other concentration safeguards as mergers and acquisitions can be reviewed by appropriate federal agencies. With regard to investment in local communities, it supported the Community Reinvestment Act (CRA) of 1977 and provisions for the applicability of state community reinvestment laws to the branches of out-of-state banks.

44. "Administration Announces Plan for Aviation Industry", *Notes on Economic Affairs*, US Information Service, 7 January 1994.

45. "Gore Proposes Reform of Communications Marketplace", *Notes on Economic Affairs*, 14 January 1994, US Information Service.

46. "Gore Offers Plan to Spur Data Superhighway", *Wall Street Journal*, 13 January 1994.

The United States' current position under the Code of Liberalisation of Capital Movements and the National Treatment Instrument

Introduction

As a signatory to the OECD Code of Liberalisation of Capital Movements (the Code) and the National Treatment Instrument (NTI), the United States has undertaken a number of obligations in the foreign direct investment field. The present annex highlights the main provisions of these instruments as well as the United States' position under them.

The OECD commitments

The Code and the NTI are the two main instruments for co-operation among OECD member countries in the field of foreign direct investment.

The Code, which has the legal status of OECD Council Decisions and is binding on all Member countries, covers the main aspects of the right of establishment for non-resident enterprises and requires OECD members to progressively liberalise their investment regimes on a non-discriminatory basis and treat resident and non-resident investors alike.

The NTI is a "policy commitment" by Member countries to accord to established foreign-controlled enterprises treatment no less favourable than that accorded to domestic enterprises in like situations. While the NTI is a non-binding agreement among OECD Member countries, all measures constituting exceptions to this principle and any other measures which have a hearing on it must be reported to the OECD.

Member countries need not, however, liberalise all their restrictions upon adherence to the above instruments. Rather, the goal of full liberalisation is to be achieved progressively over time. Accordingly, members unable to fully liberalise are permitted to maintain "reservations" to the Code of Capital Movements and "exceptions" to the NTI for outstanding foreign investment restrictions. These limitations to the liberalisation obligations may be lodged at the time a member adheres to the Codes, whenever specific obligations begin to apply to a member, or whenever new obligations are added to the instruments.

The investment obligations of the Code and the NTI are, in fact, complementary, both dealing with the laws, policies and practices of Member countries in the field of direct investment. However, the Code addresses the subject from the point of view of non-resident investors in an OECD host country, while the NTI is concerned with the rights of established foreign-controlled enterprises. Limitations on non-resident (as opposed to resident) investors affecting the enterprises' operations and other requirements set at the time of entry or establishment are covered by the Code. The investment operations of foreign-controlled enterprises after entry, including new investment, are covered by the National Treatment Instrument.

Measures pertaining to subsidiaries fall under the purview of the Code or the NTI, depending on whether they set conditions on entry/establishment or concern the activities of foreign-controlled enterprises already established. As to branches, the 1991 *Review of the OECD Declaration and Decisions on International Investment and Multinational Enterprises* introduced a distinction between "direct" branches of non-resident enterprises and "indirect" branches, that is branches of already established foreign-controlled enterprises. The latter are subject to all the five categories of measures covered by the NTI (investment by established enterprises, government procurement, official aids and subsidies, access to local financing and tax obligations). The investment activities of "direct" branches of non-resident enterprises, which concern the category of measures covered by the NTI, fall however, exclusively under the purview of the Code.

The Committee on Capital Movements and Invisible Transactions and the Committee on International Investment and Multinational Enterprises together conduct country examinations of Member country measures covered by these OECD commitments. These examinations involve a face to face discussion between representatives of the two Committees and experts from the country being examined. The discussion is based on submission by the Member concerned and a document prepared by the Secretariat. The objective is to clarify the nature and purpose of remaining restrictions and to identify possible areas for further liberalisation. The examinations usually conclude with modifications to the Member country's position and recommendations by the OECD Council to the Member's authorities concerning the future direction of the country's foreign direct investment policies.

The United States' position under the Code and the National Treatment Instrument

    a)   United States' reservations on foreign direct investment under the Code of Liberalisation of Capital Movements.

1.   "List A,   Direct investment:
     I/A

        –   In the country concerned by non-residents.

           Remark: The reservation applies only to investment in:

           i)   Atomic energy;

           ii)   Broadcasting (radio and television), common carrier, aeronautical en route, or aeronautical fixed radio station licences, unless an authorisation is granted, and the Communications Satellite Corporation;

           iii) Air transport;

           iv) Coastal and domestic shipping (including dredging and salvaging in coastal waters and transporting offshore supplies from a point within the United States to an offshore drilling rig or platform on the continental shelf);

           v)   Ocean thermal energy, hydroelectric power, geothermal steam or related resources on federal lands, mining on federal lands or on the outer continental shelf or on the deep seabed, fishing in the "Exclusive Economic Zone", and deep water ports, except through an enterprise incorporated in the United States."

2.   The United States' position under Annex E to the Code of Liberalisation of Capital Movements:

    "*i)* The acquisition by non-residents of a right-of-way for oil or gas pipelines across onshore federal lands, or a lease to develop mineral resources on onshore federal lands is subject to a reciprocity requirement;

    ii) Foreign investment in air freight forwarding and air charter activities is subject to a reciprocity requirement for US-originating traffic;

    iii) The granting of cable landing rights to non-resident firms is subject to a reciprocity requirement."

    b)   Measures reported as exceptions to the National Treatment Instrument

A. Exceptions at national level

I. Investment by established foreign-controlled enterprises

Fishing

Foreign-controlled enterprises may not engage in certain fishing operations involving coastwise trade. In addition, foreigners may not hold more than a minority of shares comprising ownership in companies owning vessels which operate in US fisheries. Also, corporate organisation requirements pertain to the registration of flag vessels for fishing in the US exclusive economic zone.

Authority: Anti-Reflagging Act (1987).

Fishing

Foreign-flag vessels may not fish or process fish in the 200 nautical mile US exclusive economic zone except under the terms of a Governing International Fisheries Agreement (GIFA), or other agreement consistent with US law.

Authority: Magnuson Fishery Conservation and Management Act (1976).

Mining, oil and gas

The Mineral Leasing Act (1920) makes public lands available for leasing only to citizens of the United States, associations of such citizens, or corporations organised under the laws of the United States, with respect to acquiring rights of way for oil pipelines, or leases or interests therein for mining coal, oil or certain other minerals. Non-US citizens may, however, own a 100 per cent interest in a US corporation that acquires a right-of-way for oil or gas pipelines across onshore federal lands, or that acquires a lease to develop mineral resources on on-shore federal lands, unless the foreign investor's home country denies similar or like privileges for the mineral or access in question to US citizens or corporations, as compared with the privileges it accords to its own citizens or corporations or to the citizens or corporations of other countries.

Authority: Mineral Land Leasing Act (1920). Chapter 3A, 10 USC §7435.

Atomic energy production

Aliens and entities owned, controlled or dominated by aliens or foreign governments may not engage in operations involving the utilisation of atomic energy. This restriction applies primarily to nuclear reactors and reprocessing plants extracting plutonium.

Authority: Atomic Energy Act. 42 USC §§2011 *et seq.* (1954).

Banking

As of August 1989, the Federal Reserve may refuse to designate as a primary dealer a foreign-controlled commercial or investment bank, if the government of the home country of the foreign bank denies national treatment to US-owned banks for government securities operations. Denial of the primary dealer designation means that the Federal Reserve, at its initiative, will no longer deal with that firm in the conduct of monetary policy. The firm, at its initiative can continue unencumbered to purchase US Government securities in government auctions.

Authority: Primary Dealers Act of 1988. 22 USC §§5341-5342.

Air transport

Cabotage and exercise of US international air route rights are reserved to national airlines controlled by US citizens, and owned 75 per cent or more (voting stock) by US citizens.

Authority: Federal Aviation Act (1958). 49 USC 41703.

Air transport: freight forwarding and charter activities

A reciprocity test on air freight forwarding and air charter activities applies any time a foreign-owned firm seeks authority to provide indirect air transportation either by cross-border or establishment for US-originating traffic. If a favourable determination is made by the Department of Transportation, indefinite registration is granted to the applicant, and subsequent applications of the same applications of the same nationality are routinely approved.

Authority: 49 USC 40109 [formerly Section 416 of the Federal Aviation Act (1958)]; 14 CFR 297, 380 Subpart F, and 48 USC App. 1485(b).

Maritime transport

The Federal Maritime Commission is authorised to take unilateral action when a foreign government, foreign carrier or other persons providing maritime-related services engages in activity that adversely affect US carriers in US oceanborne trade; creates conditions unfavourable to shipping in the foreign trade; or unduly impairs access by US-flag vessels to trade between foreign ports. Sanctions proposed under these statutes most frequently affect the cross-border provision of services, however sanctions could affect a foreign-owned investment established in the US (*e.g.* revocation of freight forwarders' licenses, suspension of preferential terminal leases).

Authority: Foreign Shipping Practices Act (1988), Merchant Marine Act (1920) Section 19, Shipping Act (1984) §13(b)4.

Telecommunications

Foreign-controlled enterprises and all other foreigners may not hold in aggregate more than 20 per cent ownership in the Communication Satellite Corporation.

Authority: Communications Satellite Act (1962). 47 USC §734(d).

Telecommunications

The Federal Communications Commission (FCC), under delegated authority from the President of the United States with concurrence of the State Department, is authorised to issue licenses to land or operate in the United States any submarine cable directly or indirectly connecting the United States with any foreign country. Under the Submarine Cable Landing Licence Act of 1921, the FCC may withhold or revoke licences if such action will assist, inter alia, in securing cable landing rights for US citizens in foreign countries.

Authority: Submarine Cable Landing Act. 47 USC §34-39.

II. Official aids and subsidies

Trans-sectoral

Eligibility for Overseas Private Investment Corporation (OPIC) insurance and guarantees for investments in eligible developing countries is limited to entities organised in the US and substantially (more than 50 per cent) beneficially owned by United States citizens, or to foreign entities at least 95 per cent owned by US citizens.

Authority: Foreign Assistance Act (1961). 22 USC §2198(c).

Trans-sectoral

To receive financial assistance under the Advanced Technology Program, a company must show that its participation will be in the economic interests of the United States, as evidenced by investments in the United States in research, development and manufacturing, and be a US-owned company or a company incorporated in the United States whose parent is incorporated in a country which *1)* affords to US-owned companies opportunities comparable to those afforded to any other company to participate in such joint ventures; *2)* affords US-owned companies local investment opportunities comparable to those afforded any other company; *3)* affords adequate and effective intellectual property rights of US-owned firms.

Authority: American Technology Pre-eminence Act of 1991. 15 USC §278N.

Trans-sectoral

To participate in the Technology Reinvestment Project (TRP), a company must conduct a significant level of its research, development, engineering, and manufacturing activities in the United States, or is US-owned company. A foreign-owned firm may be eligible if its parent company is incorporated in a country whose government encourages US-owned firms' participation in R&D consortia to which that government provides funding, and affords effective intellectual property rights for US companies.

Authority: Defense Conversion, Reinvestment and Transition Assistance Act of 1992. 10 USC §2491.

Energy

To receive financial assistance under the Energy Policy Act, a company must show that its participation will be in the economic interests of the United States, as evidenced by investments in the United States in research, development and manufacturing, and be a US-owned company or a company incorporated in the United States whose parent is incorporated in a country which *1)* affords to US-owned companies opportunities comparable to those afforded to any other company to participate in such joint ventures; *2)* affords US-owned companies local investment opportunities comparable to those afforded any other company; *3)* affords adequate and effective intellectual property rights of US-owned firms.

Authority: Energy Policy Act of 1992. 42 USC §13525.

Agriculture

Foreign-controlled US enterprises cannot obtain special government emergency loans for agricultural purposes.
Authority: 7 USC §1922. 7 USC §1941. 7 USC §1961.

III. Tax obligations

None.

IV. Government purchasing

Technical services contracting

Restrictions on eligibility for consideration by the US Agency for International Development as a contractor.
Authority: Foreign Assistance Act (1961), as amended; Agency Handbook IB.

Air transport

Foreign-controlled carriers cannot compete for Federal Government contract for the international air carriage of persons or property: *1)* between the United States and foreign points to the extent service by US. carriers is available; and *2)* between two foreign points to the extent service by US carriers is reasonably available. These prohibitions may be waived in instance where reciprocal national treatment has been negotiated on the basis of an exchange of rights or benefits of similar magnitude.

V. Access to local finance

None.

B. Exceptions by territorial subdivisions

I Investment by established foreign-controlled enterprises

California, Illinois, Iowa, Kansas, Minnesota, Missouri, Nevada, New Hampshire, New Jersey, New York, North Carolina, North Dakota, Pennsylvania, South Dakota.

Limitations on the foreign ownership of agricultural land

The following states, in addition to those noted below, have some sort of restriction on aliens owning land: California, Illinois, Kansas, Nevada, New Hampshire, New Jersey, New York, and North Carolina.

Iowa: A non-resident alien, a foreign government, or business incorporated in a foreign country or majority owned directly or indirectly by non-resident aliens, may not purchase or acquire agricultural land, with certain exceptions. Agricultural land acquired under the exceptions is subject to reporting requirements.

Minnesota: Only US citizens, permanent resident aliens, and business entities whose stock and beneficial ownership are at least 80 per cent held by US citizens or permanent resident aliens may own agricultural land.

Missouri: Non US-citizens and businesses in which non-US citizens own a controlling interest may not own agricultural land unless the non-US citizen is a resident in the US No corporation, Missouri or out-of-state, may engage in agriculture after 1975.

North Dakota: A non-US or non-Canadian citizen who is not a resident alien in the US may not hold agricultural land.

Pennsylvania: Foreign governments and non-resident non US citizens may not hold more than 100 acres of agricultural land.

South Dakota: Foreign governments and non-resident, non-US citizens may not hold more than 160 acres of agricultural land. No in or out-of-state corporation may own agricultural land.

Guam, Indiana, Oklahoma, South Carolina, Wisconsin, Wyoming, Florida, Hawaii, Idaho, Kentucky, Mississippi, Montana, Oregon.

These states have some limitation on the ownership of real property and preference in the access to – or ownership of land.

1) Real property: limitation on the ownership of real property

Guam: Alien owned businesses may only own or rent land through Guam corporations.

Indiana: Limits amount of land held by aliens. Resident and non-resident aliens may acquire real estate but must dispose of any land over 320 acres within five years of acquiring it, or the excess acreage will escheat to the state.

Oklahoma: Non-US citizens may not own real estate, in the state, with certain exceptions.

South Carolina: Non-US citizens or corporations controlled by non-US citizens may not hold more than 500 000 acres of land.

Wisconsin: Non-US citizens not resident in the US, corporations with more than 20 per cent of their stock owned by them and non-US corporations may not hold more than 640 acres of land.

Wyoming: A non-resident not eligible for citizenship may not hold real property except for personal use and not exceeding one acre.

2) Preference in the access to/or ownership of land

Florida: Non-immigrant visa holders do not receive a homestead exemption.

Hawaii: Citizens and residents of Hawaii and US military war veterans receive preference in drawings from residential and agricultural leases of state lands. Residency requirements exist for aliens and stockholders of corporations and associations who wish to rent land in designated agricultural parks.

Idaho: State land may only be sold to US citizens.

Kentucky: Real estate owned by a non-resident alien may be escheated by the State eight years following its acquisition unless: *a)* the alien becomes a US citizen, *b)* they have declared their intent to become US citizens; or *c)* the corporations are organised under state law.

Mississippi: Non-resident aliens may not hold land longer than 20 years before becoming a US citizen except that they may acquire 320 acres for industrial development and 5 acres for residential purposes. Moreover, a non-resident alien may not purchase public land, except that they may purchase 320 acres of public land for industrial purposes and 5 acres for residential purposes.

Montana: State lands may only be sold to US citizens, those who have declared their intent to become US citizens or corporations organised under state law.

Oregon: State lands may only be sold to US citizens or those who have declared their intent to become US citizens.

Montana

Mining

Montana has a reciprocity test for coal leases on state owned land.

Alabama, Arkansas, California, Connecticut, Delaware, Florida, Georgia, Illinois, Iowa, Maryland, Michigan, Minnesota, Mississippi, North Carolina, Texas, Virginia, Washington, Wisconsin

Banking: Operational restrictions

Alabama, Arkansas, Florida, Georgia, Minnesota, Mississippi, North Carolina, Virginia and Wisconsin effectively prohibit US affiliates of non-US banks from acquiring in-state banks by requiring an acquiring bank to have its ''home state'' or ''principal place of business'' in a state of a regional banking pact where the majority of its consolidated deposits is located.

California: Deposit agencies of non-US banks are prohibited from accepting deposits other than from a foreign nation or a person domiciled in a foreign nation. State chartered banks and out-of-state US banks owned by non-US banks are treated differently than other California or US banks in acquisition of a California bank.

Connecticut: Banking corporations organised under the laws of another country cannot maintain an office in the State to solicit deposits or conduct a general banking business.

Delaware: Non-US banks may maintain only one office and may not act in a manner to attract customers from the general public. They may not act as a fiduciary of any sort nor accept deposits from US persons, unless they could do so if operating in the state as a federal agency under the International Banking Act.

Florida: Non-US banks may not establish full service branches or banks. Non-US bank agencies may not accept domestic deposits or act as fiduciary. Out-of-State banks may not establish full service branches.

Illinois: Banking corporations shall be licensed to transact business in the State. Non-US banks organised in a foreign country may have one bank office in the central Chicago business district.

Iowa: Banks organised under the laws of a foreign country or a part of the US not a state or DC may not acquire Iowa banks or bank holding companies.

Maryland: A person who is not a US citizen may not directly or indirectly control state savings and loan associations.

Mississippi: Upon approval and licensing by the State Banking Board, foreign banking corporations shall be limited to transactions that are clearly limited to and are usual in international or foreign business and financing international commerce, shall be unable to exercise fiduciary powers and unable to receive deposits. For a foreign banking corporation the first application fee shall be a minimum of two thousand five hundred dollars ($2 500) and a maximum of ten thousand dollars ($10 000), annual licence renewal shall be two hundred fifty dollars ($250).

North Carolina: A bank or bank holding company within the state can only be acquired by a bank holding company from the South Eastern Region (14 states and DC).

Texas: A foreign bank agency must be located in a county of at least 1.5 million people. Deposits can be accepted and loans made only through the bank, not the agency.

Washington: Non-US bank branches may not have more than one office in the state. Branches are effectively prohibited from accepting initial deposits of less than $100 000 from US citizens. Non-US banks may not hold real estate other than as a place of business or residence for its employees, incidental to its loan business. Non-US banks may not acquire already established financial institutions, nor shall their officers serve as directors. Non-US bank agencies are effectively limited to international business.

Florida, Illinois, New Jersey, Pennsylvania, Texas, Washington

Banking: Reciprocity conditions

Florida: Establishment of an agency or representative office by non-US Bank is conditioned on reciprocity.

Illinois: Non-US bank corporations cannot be given a certificate of authority to transact business unless Illinois or other US banks are accorded similar privileges in the non-US bank's home country, or pays a special $50 000 annual "reciprocal fee".

New Jersey: Limits may be placed on the amount of a New Jersey bank that a non-US person owning more than 25 per cent of a non-US bank may acquire. Under special circumstances, a bank holding company organised out-of-state, but non-US owned, may acquire New Jersey banks or bank holding companies on a reciprocal basis.

Pennsylvania: The state banking department may deny to non-US banks permission to operate in the state in the absence of reciprocity for US banks in the country in which the non-US bank is domiciled.

Texas: An agency of a bank organised in a foreign country may be denied a licence to operate in Texas if that country denied Texas banks the ability to operate there, and if denial is in the public interest.

Authority: Illinois: Revised Statute, Ch. 17, para. 270. New Jersey: Statutes 17.9(A). Pennsylvania: Statutes 105B (8.1). Texas; Rev. Cit. Stat. Ann. Articles 342-1006.

Tennessee, North Carolina, North Dakota

Insurance: Licensing

These states do not issue a licence to foreign government owned or controlled insurance companies.

Colorado, Connecticut, Florida, Idaho, Illinois, Indiana, Minnesota, Nebraska, New York, Ohio, Oklahoma, Washington, Wisconsin

Insurance: Reciprocity provisions

These states have reciprocity laws enabling insurance Commissioners to retaliate against perceived unfair insurance trade rules in other countries.

Alabama, Arkansas, Arizona, California, Connecticut, Florida, Hawaii, Idaho, Illinois, Indiana, Iowa, Kansas, Maine, Maryland, Massachusetts, Michigan, Minnesota, Missouri, New Jersey, New Mexico, North Carolina, Oregon, Rhode Island, Virginia, Wisconsin

Insurance: Surplus fund requirements

US branches of non-US firms are required to maintain surplus funds in excess of deposits; these "trusteed surplus" funds are usually held in trust by either a state or a US-incorporated trustee such as a local bank or Port-of-Entry State bank.

II.   Official aids and subsidies

Hawaii, North Carolina

Agriculture

Hawaii, restricts State agricultural loans to Hawaii corporations with at least 75 per cent of each class of stock owned by US citizens who have resided in the state for five years. North Carolina excludes non-US citizens from its Farm Ownership Loan Program.

Florida

Trans-sectoral

Foreign persons may not qualify for Small Business Administration loans.

III. Tax obligations

Montana

Trans-sectoral

Small businesses with a non-resident shareholder may not take the Montana small business income tax credit.

Authority: Montana Tax Code 15-31-123.

IV. Government purchasing

None.

V. Access to local finance

None.

c) Measures reported for transparency at the National Treatment Instrument

A. Transparency measures at the level of National Government

I. Measures based on public order and essential security considerations

a) *Investment by established foreign controlled enterprises*

Trans-sectoral

Under the US Omnibus Trade and Competitiveness Act, the President has the power to block a foreign acquisition which threatens to impair the national security. The President may use this power only if the President finds, after an investigation, that:

1) there is credible evidence leading him to believe that the foreign interest might take action that threatens to impair the national security, and *2)* other provisions of law (*e.g.* antitrust laws, Export Administration Act, Defence Production Act, International Trade in Armaments Regulations) other than the International Emergency Economic Powers Act do not in his judgement provide adequate and appropriate authority to protect the national security.

Authority: Defence Production Act (1950), Section 721, as added by §5021 of the Omnibus Trade and Competitiveness Act (1988), and as amended by §837 of the National Defence Authorisation Act for Fiscal Year 1993. 50 USC App. 2170.

Air transport

Cabotage reserved to national airlines at least 75 per cent owned by US citizens. Also, there are citizenship requirements for management and board of directors.

Authority: Federal Aviation Act (1958). 49 USC 41703.

Maritime services

Foreign-controlled enterprises may not engage in dredging or salvaging.

Authority: Act of 28 May 1906, Section 1, as amended (46 USC App. 292).

Maritime transport

Foreign-controlled enterprises may not acquire, mortgage or charter vessels owned by a US citizen, documented under US law, or last documented under US law without the approval of the Secretary of Transportation. In times of war or national emergency this provision extends to shipyard facilities and controlling interests in corporations owning such facilities or US flag vessels.

Authority: 46 USC App. 1241, 1241-1.

Maritime transport

Cabotage reserved to ships owned by US citizens or companies with minimum 75 per cent ownership by US citizens.

Authority: Jones Act, Section 27 of the Merchant Marine Act (1920).

Maritime transport

Products exported pursuant to US Government loan for this purpose restricted to national flag.

Authority: 46 USC App. 1241,1241-1.

Maritime transport

Transport of military supplies and personal effects of military and civilian employees reserved to national flag.

Authority: Cargo Preference Act of 1904 (10 USC 2631).

Radio and television, communications

For radio, broadcasting, and telephone companies in regard to common carrier radio licences, US enterprises with foreign ownership exceeding 20 per cent, aliens, and foreign corporations may not be granted the relevant licence. When a corporation is directly or indirectly controlled by another corporation, the Federal Communications Commission may refuse to approve a licence if more than a 25 per cent interest in the controlling company is foreign and if the Commission finds it in the public interest to do so. There are additional restrictions on the nationality of management that apply in the case of broadcasting companies, and telephone companies having a common carrier radio licence.

Authority: Communications Act of 1934. 47 USC §§151 *et seq.*, see particularly §§310(b).

b) Corporate organisation

Communications

Under a 1984 law, the Department of Commerce is authorised to aware a contract, through a competitive process, to a "United States private sector party" for the marketing of data from the government-owned "Landsat" system, as well as for the development and operation of a new civil and remote sensing system. A firm's eligibility for the contract awarded is predicated upon its key management and a majority of its Directors being US citizens, as well as it having a US corporate headquarters and having filed a US tax return in previous years.

Authority: Land Remote Sensing Commercialisation Act 1984. 15 USC §§4212, 4222.

c) *Government purchasing*

Defence

Foreign-controlled enterprises operating in the United States may not be granted a contract or subcontract involving classified information, except under special arrangements to be determined on a case-by-case basis.

Authority: US Dept. of Defence Regulation 5200.22-R, Sect. II; Executive Order 10865, 12064.

Air transport

Foreign-controlled carriers cannot compete for Federal Government contracts for international air carriage of persons or property, except in limited instances between two foreign points.

Authority: Federal Aviation Act (1958).

d) *Official aids and subsidies*

Maritime transport

Foreign-controlled enterprises may not: *1)* obtain loan guarantees or tax deferment benefits for the financing or re-financing of the cost of purchasing, constructing or operating commercial vessels or gear, or obtain war risk insurance; *2)* sell obsolete vessels to the Secretary of Transportation in exchange for credit towards new vessels; *3)* hold a preferred ship mortgage (however foreign-controlled corporations may have a preferred ship mortgage as long as a US citizen trustee holds the mortgage for their benefit); *4)* purchase vessels converted by the government for commercial use or surplus war-built vessels at a special statutory sales price; *5)* obtain construction-differential or operating-differential subsidies for vessel construction or operation.

Authority: Merchant Marine Act (1936), Merchant Ship Sales Act (1946).

II. Other measures reported for transparency at the level of National Government

a) Investment by established foreign controlled enterprises

Trans-sectoral

To engage in certain activities, a foreign-controlled enterprise operating in the United States must meet certain requirements relating to the form of its business organisation. For example, a foreign-controlled enterprise must incorporate under the laws of one of the States of the United States in order to obtain licences to: *1)* construct dams, reservoirs, power facilities and transmission lines; or *2)* mine uranium. Similar state-level measures exist in some states.

Authority: 16 USC §797.

b) Corporate organisation

Energy

There are corporate organisation requirements, defining "US citizen", for a licence to own, construct or operate: *1)* an ocean thermal energy conversion (OTEC) facility located in US territorial waters, documented under US laws, or connected to the US by pipeline or cable; or *2)* a moving OTEC plant ship wherever located. The president or other executive officer and the chairman of the board of directors must be US citizens and the board of directors must have no more foreign citizens servicing as directors than a minority of the number necessary to constitute a quorum. In addition, there is a reciprocity provision for plant ships in the Ocean Thermal Energy Conversion Act.

Authority: Ocean Thermal Energy Conversion Act (1980). Section 1. 42 USC §9111, 42 USC §9102(18).

Banking

A majority of the directors of a national bank that is an affiliate or subsidiary of a foreign bank must be US citizens.

Authority: The National Bank Act. 12 USC §72.

Customs brokerages

To obtain a licence to operate a customs brokerage, one officer or partner of a firm must be a licensed customs broker and a US citizen.

Authority: Tariff Act (1930), 19 USC §1641(b).

c)   Government purchasing

None.

B.   Measures reported for transparency at the level of territorial subdivisions

a)   Investment by established foreign controlled enterprises

Ohio

Agricultural Land: Reporting requirements

Non-resident, non-US citizens foreign governments and entities controlled by foreigners organised in/or having their principal place of business in foreign nations and holding an interest in agricultural land, must file a disclosure statement with the state.

Authority: Revised Statutes, Chapter 442.

Nebraska

Agriculture

Neither foreign nor out-of-state firms may engage in farming or ranching.

Authority: Constitution of Nebraska, Article 12, paragraph 8(1).

Illinois, Massachusetts, Florida, South Dakota

Fishing

These states regulate in some way commercial fishing by vessels owned by out-of-state residents. Most such states distinguish between state and out-of-state residents. For example, regarding commercial freshwater fishing, an alien or other non-resident must pay $500 for a permit, while a comparable licence fee for a resident is $40. In a few states foreigners' operations are regulated explicitly.

Hawaii

Hunting and fishing

Only resident of the state may obtain a licence for the purpose of importing game birds for a private or commercial shooting game preserve.

Authority: Revised Statutes, Section 183D-34, 35.

Rhode Island, Connecticut

Manufacturing – Public utilities

Rhode Island: No public utility shall sell its product in the State unless it has received a certificate from the State. The certificate shall only be given to a resident and citizen of the state or an association, all of whose members are residents and citizens of the state, or to a corporation created by a special act of the General Assembly.

Connecticut: Out-of-state electric companies must notify State officials and fulfil certain requirements before owning and operating an electric utility.

Authority: Rhode Island: Section 39-3-1, -2. Connecticut: General Statute, Section 16-246C (1989).

Connecticut, Guam, Oregon

Banking

Connecticut: In order to acquire a Connecticut banking institution, all-out-of-state banks must meet prudential requirements and be from jurisdictions which allow Connecticut banks to acquire domestic banks on terms no less restrictive than imposed by Connecticut.

Guam: Non-territory banks received branch privileges similar to those given to a Guam bank in their jurisdiction.

Oregon: To hold property in trust, out-of-state banking firms must be incorporated or domiciled in a jurisdiction that allows Oregon banks to hold property in trust. A grandfather clause applies.

Authority: Connecticut: General Statutes Sec. 36-35; Public Act 90-2. Guam: Civil Code. Oregon: Revised Statutes, Section 713.010-.110.

Rhode Island

Banking: Asset requirements

A building and loan association incorporated out-of-state must have assets over US$100 000.

Authority: Statute, Section 19-24-1 to 6.

Minnesota, South Dakota, Massachusetts, Nebraska, New Jersey, New York, Pennsylvania, Rhode Island, Texas, Virginia

Banking: Authorisation/Notification

Minnesota: Non-resident (foreign and out-of-state) banks must be chartered under the laws of Minnesota to do business.

South Dakota: Special requirements apply to the acquisition of shares in a bank by out-of-state bank holding companies. An out-of-state bank may not acquire shares, whereas a foreign bank not established in another state is considered as a South Dakota bank for the purpose of acquiring shares.

Massachusetts: Out-of-state banks must file a certificate to transact business, as do banks from other New England state.

Nebraska: All State chartered banks doing business in the State must be organised under Nebraska laws. Banks organised under 12 USC 21 et. seq. are not bound by this requirement.

New Jersey: Banks doing business in the State must be established in accordance with New Jersey State law.

New York: Non US Banks with world wide assets of under $500 million must apply for a licence to maintain a representative office. Those with over $500 million assets need only register.

Pennsylvania: Non US Banks require written permission from the Department of Banking to establish offices.

Rhode Island: Building and loan associations must provide certain information to be licensed.

Texas: Agencies of bank corporations not organised in the US must register and obtain a licence from the State and may only maintain one office in the State.

Virginia: No foreign corporation that does not meet the requirements of Virginia law can engage in banking or in the trust business.

Most states (exceptions listed below)

Insurance: Demonstrated experience requirements

Most states require new applicants for insurance licences to have demonstrated up to five years of successful insurance experience in another jurisdiction before their application can be considered. Some state waive this requirement for companies that are newly incorporated in their state, judging the new applicant on the grounds of solvency and business experience in other fields. All states treat US branches admitted to the US market through their own state in the same manner as they treat locally incorporated companies. Firms incorporated in another sate and US branches of non-US firms admitted to the US market through another US state are required to meet seasoning requirements that may have slightly longer time frames. Many states give insurance Commissioners the authority to modify or waive these requirements under certain conditions. The states which do not have such seasoning requirements are: Georgia, Idaho, Indiana, Louisiana, Michigan, Missouri, Montana, Nevada, Ohio, Oklahoma and Rhode Island. In addition, Oregon, Texas and Wisconsin impose seasoning requirements only as a matter of reciprocity, *i.e.* when the home state of the applying firm imposes such requirements.

California, Connecticut, Florida, Iowa, Kansas, Michigan, Montana, New Jersey, North Carolina, North Dakota, Oregon, Pennsylvania

Insurance: Deposit requirements

The above states treat out-of-state firms (*i.e.* incorporated in another state or outside the US) differently from in-state firms with respect to deposit requirements:

California: Deposits for US branches are the same regardless of their port-of-entry state.

Connecticut: US branches must maintain assets in the US equal to their US liabilities, plus minimum capital and surplus requirements. Foreign and alien life insurance companies must maintain a surplus fund of not less than $3 million.

Florida/Iowa/Louisiana/South Carolina: Deposit amounts are the same for domestic companies and US branches admitted to the US market through the state in question, but deposit amounts are different for foreign companies and US branches admitted through other states.

Kansas: US branches must have $100 000 in excess of all their liabilities in the US for unpaid losses and other liabilities.

Michigan: Domestic companies must deposit $300 000. US branches entered through Michigan must have trusteed assets. Foreign companies and US branches that enter through other states are not required to make an additional deposit. However, they may be subject to retaliatory provisions.

Montana: Foreign and alien companies must maintain deposits that are four times higher than domestic ones. Non resident insurers which have transacted insurance for less than five years in the United States must maintain an additional surplus in Montana to do business in the state.

New Jersey: Deposits are the same for all non-life companies. For life and health companies, deposit amounts for domestic companies are different for those for foreign companies and US branches admitted through another state.

North Carolina: Deposit requirements are lower for domestic companies than for foreign and alien companies. US branches must also have total statutory deposits in the US equal to the normal capital required for admission into insurance business in the state.

North Dakota: foreign and alien companies must indicate the amount and location of deposits within the US.

Oregon: There are no deposit requirements for domestic companies. A $100 000 to $260 000 deposit is required for foreign and alien companies on some types of insurance.

Pennsylvania: Special capitalisation requirements apply to foreign life insurance companies.

Alabama, Alaska, Arkansas, California, Colorado, Connecticut, Delaware, Florida, Georgia, Hawaii, Idaho, Kansas, Maryland, Montana, Nevada, New Mexico, New York, Oklahoma, Oregon, Pennsylvania, Rhode Island, South Dakota, West Virginia, Washington, Wyoming

Insurance: Licensing

These states do not issue a licence to any government owned insurance company. These restrictions apply to all out of State government owned companies, not solely those owned by foreign interests.

Illinois, Massachusetts, New Jersey, New York, Pennsylvania

Insurance: Reviews

These states issue continuous licences for insurance companies incorporated in their state but require periodic review for licences issued to other companies; in general, renewal is automatic unless a firm has unpaid premium taxes or other similar problems.

Some States

Maritime transport

Some states may restrict the operation of vessels by aliens (and out-of-state residents) through higher licence fees than those paid by state residents.

b) Tax obligations

Hawaii

Real Estate

As of January 1991, persons who are not residents of Hawaii and who sell Hawaii real property are subject to income tax withholding.

Authority: Act 213, Hawaii Sess. Laws.

Rhode Island

Banking

Building and loan associations incorporated out of state must pay a tax of 25 per cent of the difference between their deposits and investments in the state.

Authority: Statute 19.24.1 to 6.

c)   Corporate organisation

Connecticut, Hawaii, Maryland, Michigan, Missouri, New Jersey, North Carolina, South Dakota

Banking: Residency requirements

Connecticut: At least three-quarters of the members of the governing board of a state bank and trust company must be residents of the state.

Hawaii: At least three of the directors of any bank must be residents of Hawaii at the time of their election and during their term of office.

Maryland: Only Maryland citizens who are US citizens may act as incorporators of state banks, trust companies, savings banks and savings and loan associations.

Michigan: Incorporators have to be US citizens.

Missouri: Non-resident (out-of-state and non-US) persons may not act as a trustee on a deed of trust or conveyance unless a qualified Missouri person is named as co-trustee.

New Jersey: The incorporators and directors of savings and loan associations organised in New Jersey must be US citizens.

North Carolina: Three-quarters of the directors of banks under state banking laws must be residents of North Carolina.

South Dakota: Three-quarters of a bank's board of directors must be US citizens. Moreover, the incorporators of a bank and the majority of the incorporators of a savings and loans association must reside in the state. Two-thirds of the bank's board of directors must be residents in the state and a majority must reside within 100 miles of the place of business. A majority of the board of a savings and loan association ust be state residents.

Alabama, Alaska, Arizona, Arkansas, Florida, Georgia, Hawaii, Idaho, Illinois, Indiana, Iowa, Kansas, Kentucky, Louisiana, Maryland, Massachusetts, Michigan, Minnesota, Mississippi, Missouri, Montana, Nebraska, Nevada, New Hampshire, New York, North Carolina, Ohio, Oklahoma, Oregon, Pennsylvania, South Dakota, Tennessee, Texas, Utah, Vermont, Washington, Wyoming

Insurance

In the states, the incorporators, officer and/or directors of companies incorporated in the state and/or entering through another must meet citizenship and/or residency requirements.

Florida

Trans-sectoral

Both Florida and out-of-state corporations that own real estate must maintain an office and registered agent in the state.

Authority: Florida State. 607.0505 (1989)

All states

Trans-sectoral – Registration, agent/office requirements

In conformity with the Model Business Corporation Act, all states, Puerto Rico and DC require out of jurisdiction corporations to obtain a certificate of authority to transact business in the jurisdiction. Arkansas, Kansas, Massachusetts, Nevada and Puerto Rico require certain filings by out of jurisdiction corporations, but do not provide specifically for a certificate to be issued. All jurisdictions, except Connecticut, Puerto Rico, Massachusetts, Maryland, New York, Oregon, Pennsylvania and West Virginia require out of jurisdiction corporations to maintain a registered principal office and a registered agent in the state. Maryland, Puerto Rico and Virginia require the agent to be either an individual or an in-state corporation.

Authority: Model Business Corporation Act, annotated third addition.

c)   *Government purchasing*

None.

Annex 2

The Exon-Florio provision

1. Background

In 1988, in reaction to Congressional concerns that the President, short of invoking emergency powers, had no authority to prohibit foreign acquisition of US companies, the Defense Production Act was amended to add section 721 to provide such authority in certain circumstances to protect national security. While retaining power to prohibit or suspend acquisitions, the President delegated authority to the Committee on Foreign Investment in the United States (CFIUS) to "receive notices and other information, to determine whether investigation should be undertaken, and to make investigations". Section 721 is commonly known as the Exon-Florio provision. Final implementing regulations were published in November 1991.

In 1991, the Defense Production Act was amended to ensure that the Exon-Florio provision did not expire when its parent legislation periodically lapsed. Exon-Florio was again amended in 1992, when technological leadership (in areas affecting national security) was added as a factor to be considered in transactions. The amendment also required a full investigation when an entity which is government-controlled proposes a transaction that "could affect national security". Another 1992 change included a requirement that Congress receive a written report when the President makes a determination on a transaction, whether or not the transaction has been prohibited or suspended. These changes, whose implementing regulations were published in May 1994, followed the proposed purchase of a defense company by a foreign government-owned entity.

2. Main features

The principal features of the Exon-Florio provision, as set out in the amended section 721 of the Defence Production Act 1950, and amended in the National Defense Authorisation Act for FY1993 are as follows.

111

First, the law gives the President authority under certain circumstances to suspend or prohibit or to take other action with respect to any acquisition by or with foreign entities of an enterprise engaged in interstate commerce in the United States.

Second, the law provides for a two-stage review and investigation procedure before action may be taken by the President. The "review" or "notice" phase is to be completed within 30 days from the receipt of written notification of a proposed acquisition. During this phase, a decision will be taken on whether the proposed investment raises any national security concerns or whether any national security implications should be explored further by investigation. An investigation is obligatory in any instance in which an entity controlled by or acting on behalf of a foreign government seeks to engage in a transaction which could result in foreign control and affect US national security. At the conclusion of the "investigation" phase, which must not exceed 45 days, a report and recommendation will be sent to the President. The President must announce his decision to suspend or prohibit the transaction within 15 days. Accordingly, the entire procedure may not exceed 90 days. In each case referred to the President for decision, the President must submit to the Congress his determination whether or not to take action, including a detailed explanation of his findings and the factors considered.

Third, Exon-Florio empowers the President to take appropriate action to prohibit or suspend transactions, if he finds that:

    i) There is credible evidence to believe that the foreign interests exercising control might take action that threatens to impair the national security; and

    ii) Existing laws, other than the International Emergency Economic Powers Act and the Exon-Florio provision, do not provide adequate and appropriate legal authority to protect the national security.

Fourth, the factors to be considered in judging any particular investment, taking into account the requirements of national security, may include the following:

- domestic production needed for projected national defense requirements;
- the capability and capacity of domestic industries to meet national defense requirements, including the availability of human resources, products, technology, materials, and other supplies and services; and
- the control of domestic industries and commercial activity by foreign citizens as it affects the capability and capacity of the United States to meet the requirements of national security; and
- the potential effects of the proposed or pending transaction on United States international technological leadership in areas affecting United States national security;
- the potential effects on proliferation of military goods, equipment or technology to certain countries.

3. The executive order and the role of CFIUS

Executive Order 12661 of 27 December 1988 provides for the implementation of the Omnibus Trade Act of 1988. The main elements of the Order concerning the Exon-Florio provision are as follows:

- CFIUS is assigned the task of receiving notifications, reviewing and investigating individual cases, and advising the President in the exercise of his authority.
- If any member of CFIUS disagrees with a decision not to undertake an investigation, the chairman of CFIUS must seek the President's guidance no later than 25 days after receiving written notification of the case, *i.e.* at least 5 days before a decision must be taken under the law on whether to proceed with an investigation.
- If on completion of an investigation CFIUS is unable to make a unanimous recommendation to the President, the differing views and issues will be submitted to the President for his decision.
- The Attorney-General and the Director of Office Management and Budget become members of CFIUS, which already comprised the Secretaries of the Departments of Treasury, State, Defense, Commerce, the Special Trade Representative, and the Chairman of the Council of Economic Advisors. In September 1993, the Director of the Office of Science and Technology, the Assistant to the President for National Security Affairs, and the Assistant to the President for Economic Policy were added. (Other agencies, *e.g.* Energy, Interior and Transportation, may be asked to participate in the review and investigation process.)
- The chairman of CFIUS (Treasury), in consultation with other members of the Committee, is delegated authority to issue regulations to implement the new law.

4. Implementing regulations

Within the framework of the law, the regulations create a voluntary system of notification of acquisitions. The regulations specify who should give notice and provide guidance as to the kinds of transactions that should be notified. They also define a number of key terms, such as "acquisition", "foreign interest" and "control". "National security" is not defined. Finally, the regulations set forth the procedures to be followed by CFIUS in the exercise of its review and investigation function, and spell out the actions including divestment that could be ordered by the President.

– *Who should notify?*

Notification of an acquisition under the regulations may be made by a party to the transaction or by any member agency of CFIUS. The Committee will not accept notices from third parties, although any person might contact the Committee to inform it about a particular transaction. All information provided to the United States authorities is kept in confidence and exempt from the Freedom of Information Act. Disclosure may only be made in connection with administrative or judicial actions or proceedings, or to the United States Congress.

– *Transactions to be notified*

Only transactions and proposed transactions that result or could result in foreign control of a United States enterprise are subject to the Exon-Florio provision. A "foreign person" is a foreign national or an entity subject to control by foreign interests. "Foreign control" means that a foreign person has, or will have, the power to determine important matters relating to a United States entity by virtue of significant stock ownership, contractual arrangements or other means.

Certain investment transactions are excluded from the regulations' coverage, notably "greenfield" investments and acquisitions of United States enterprises operating entirely outside the United States. The acquisition of assets that do not constitute an ongoing business are also excluded as are acquisitions of voting securities "solely for the purpose of investment" and amounting to 10 per cent or less of the voting securities of the United States enterprise.

While "national security" is not defined, earlier regulations published in November 1991 stated that notification of an acquisition would be clearly appropriate when, for example, the United States enterprise being acquired provides "products or key technologies essential to the United States defense industrial base". By contrast, notification would not be expected where the entire output of the company being acquired consists of "products and/or services that clearly have no relation to national security, *e.g.* toys and games; food products; hotels and restaurants; or legal services".

There is no negative list of products considered not essential to the national security, because it is felt that such a list would not provide guidance sufficiently detailed to be helpful to the parties, and could reduce the President's discretion in protecting the national security. Similarly, there is no threshold value of a transaction over which investors should notify the government, because it is felt that the relationship between a transaction's size and its impact on national security is too unpredictable. Therefore investors must exercise their own judgement in determining whether a transaction may affect the national security. General guidance may be obtained, however, by contacting the chair of CFIUS.

– *CFIUS procedures*

The timetable for review and investigation of notifications is laid down in the statute. CFIUS, however, may determine whether a particular notice is in accordance with the regulations and may reject non-conforming notices. It may also call for additional information during the course of a review or investigation; for example, in the case where one party has not provided information to complete the notification (most often in the case of hostile transactions). In the event that a party to the acquisition has submitted false or misleading information, or has omitted material information, CFIUS may reopen its review.

– *Possible actions by the President*

Upon receipt of a CFIUS report, the President may suspend or prohibit a pending acquisition by foreign interests. In the case of completed transactions, he may seek other remedies including action for divestment, provided such action is based on the situation at the time the transaction was concluded. Divestment is not available as a remedy for notified transactions if CFIUS has previously decided not to undertake an investigation, or if the President has previously decided against exercising his authority in regard to the acquisition in question. For non-notified transactions, however, the possibility of divestment remains, and there is no time limit on the President's power to divest non-notified transactions. After a three-year period, an agency cannot give notice with respect to a completed transaction, but the CFIUS Chairman can still, in consultation with Committee members, an investigation of transactions raising serious national security concerns, thereby preserving the President's authority.

Annex 3

Statistics on foreign direct investment in the United States

Table 1. US Business enterprises acquired or established by foreign direct investors

Total value of transactions and number of investments 1986-1992

	1986	1987	1988	1989	1990	1991	1992
All investments (million US$)	39 177	40 310	72 692	71 163	65 932	25 538	13 469
Number	1 040	978	1 424	1 580	1 617	1 091	690
Acquisitions (million US$)	31 450	33 933	64 855	59 708	55 315	17 806	10 191
Number	555	543	869	837	839	561	360
Establishments (million US$)	7 728	6 377	7 837	11 455	10 617	7 732	3 278
Number	485	435	555	743	778	530	330

Notes: – Data is from BEA's annual survey of new Foreign Direct Investment in the US (FDIUS) which covers: 1) existing US businesses wherein foreign investors acquired at least a 10 per cent voting interest; and 2) new US business enterprises established by foreign investors.
   – Foreign-source funds used to acquire or establish US affiliates are also included in US capital flows for FDIUS. However, because the total FDIUS capital flows also include funds that are used for other purposes, the two measures are not directly comparable.

Source: Survey of Current Business, Bureau of Economic Analysis, US Department of Commerce, May 1993

Tableau 2. **Foreign direct investment flows by country, 1981-1992**

Million US$

	1981	1982	1983	% of total	1984	1985	1986	1987	1988	1989	% of total	1990	1991	1992	% of total
OECD AREA	20 256	11 009	10 932	94.9	23 819	18 832	34 717	61 003	53 586	63 375	91.8	43 451	25 777	2 393	70.6
Europe	14 887	10 448	8 919	77.4	14 890	13 521	22 527	46 291	31 864	43 085	62.4	21 543	12 936	−46	−1.4
EEC	14 234	9 585	7 682	66.7	13 504	10 513	19 855	42 314	31 032	35 700	51.7	20 836	11 489	−1 939	−57.2
Belgium-Luxembourg	297	81	305	2.6	415	−203	638	340	142	976	1.4	1 966	−1 617	953	28.1
France	1 961	−220	−133	−1.2	776	35	980	3 155	3 122	2 744	4.0	5 987	4 462	−468	−13.8
Germany	1 702	473	1 011	8.8	1 219	2 056	2 186	4 591	2 245	3 738	5.4	585	2 167	1 389	41.0
Ireland	32	2	79	0.7	61	..	..	100	295	1 008	1.5	−138	475	390	11.5
Italy	395	314	21	0.2	321	68	74	−21	−683	850	1.2	429	−175	−250	−7.4
Netherlands	5 223	3 686	2 662	23.1	3 381	2 877	4 375	8 413	6 137	7 323	10.6	7 163	1 006	−1 491	−44.0
Spain	23	93	−30	−0.3	39	64	76	76	63	90	0.1	188	373	112	3.3
United Kingdom	4 512	5 103	3 730	32.4	7 184	5 198	11 319	25 627	19 617	18 939	27.4	4 519	4 382	−2 608	−77.0
Other Europe	653	863	1 237	10.7	1 386	3 008	2 672	3 977	832	7 385	10.7	707	1 447	1 893	55.9
Sweden	10	38	339	2.9	159	249	1 373	746	−95	587	0.9	443	274	1 381	40.8
Swizerland	500	898	833	7.2	1 107	2 448	1 295	3 083	831	5 184	7.5	−633	1 490	528	15.6
North America	2 127	−1 516	170	1.5	3 435	774	2 526	4 336	1 852	1 793	2.6	1 821	2 383	−2	−63.3
Canada	2 127	−1 516	170	1.5	3 435	774	2 526	4 336	1 852	1 793	2.6	1 821	2 383	−2	−63.3
Other OECD countries	3 242	2 077	1 843	16.0	5 494	4 537	9 664	10 376	19 870	18 497	26.8	20 087	10 458	4 583	135.3
Australia	248	128	198	1.7	1 180	1 155	2 606	1 457	2 741	−81	−0.1	1 279	−200	663	19.6
Japan	2 970	1 952	1 644	14.3	4 358	3 368	7 031	8 806	17 205	18 653	27.0	18 754	10 660	3 960	116.9
NON OECD AREA	5 077	2 801	586	5.1	1 748	1 658	1 428	−1 422	4 985	5 635	8.2	4 971	−331	995	29.4
Africa	..	..	..	..	..	..	..	49	−41	55	0.1	−8	90	−6	−0.2
Latin America-															
Caribbean	2 116	1 895	348	3.0	520	1 243	965	−2 374	2 944	4 069	5.9	5 199	−1 513	841	24.8
Argentina	79	47	64	0.6	43	42	11	29	−14	79	0.1	50	−48	68	2.0
Brazil	..	110	−	−	76	40	−16	70	−8	145	0.2	−46	97	21	0.6
Mexico	28	95	−39	−0.3	61	222	322	22	38	107	0.2	224	132	476	14.0
Middle East	2 660	168	−53	−0.5	−18	55	−171	302	1 378	900	1.3	−613	465	4	0.1
Israel	−12	24	7	0.1	47	12	3	−14	−56	15	0.0	5	500	−23	−0.7
Saudi Arabia	12	10	7	0.1	−1	−6	7	−25	1 508	611	0.9	−613	−213	2	0.1
South and South															
East Asia	25	..	..	..	..	..	..	649	710	819	1.2	385	521	85	2.5
DAEs	14	28	5	0.0	26	−17	76	550	737	487	0.7	361	540	51	1.5
Hong Kong	31	57	20	0.2	48	33	82	456	88	388	0.6	259	339	5	0.1
Korea	31	−40	−32	−0.3	−35	−53	−16	−136	353	−821	−1.2	−698	333	46	1.4
Singapore	−66	1	6	0.1	6	6	4	139	119	471	0.7	370	−419	−22	−0.6
Taiwan	13	10	12	0.1	6	−1	13	71	131	421	0.6	356	312	7	0.2
Other Asia	11	..	−	..	..	..	..	99	−27	332	0.5	24	−19	34	1.0
Indonesia	..	−	−	−	−	−1	−7	−4	26	17	0.0	−13	2	36	1.1
Other countries	276	..	..	..	..	..	..	−56	−4	−200	−0.3	−4	−6	2	0.1
TOTAL	25 333	13 810	11 518	100.0	25 567	20 490	36 145	59 581	58 571	69 010	100.0	48 422	25 446	3 388	100.0

Source : United States Department of Commerce, Bureau of Economic Analysis: Survey of Current Business, various issues.

Chart 1. **Foreign direct investment flows by country**

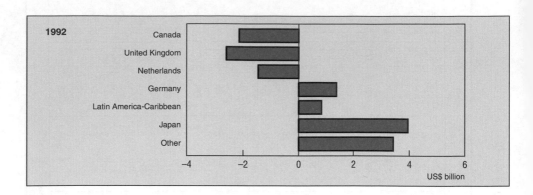

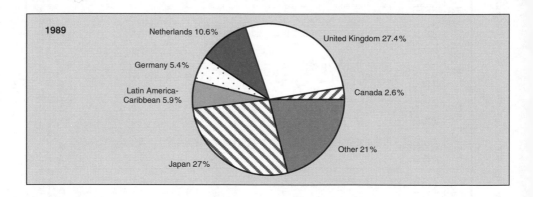

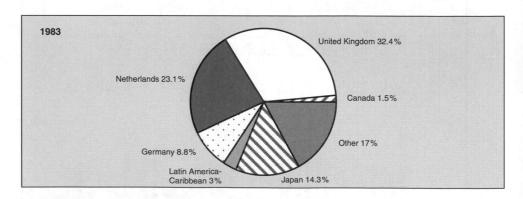

Source: OECD/DAF.

120

Table 3. **Foreign direct investment flows by industry, 1981-1992**

Million US$

	1981	1982	1983	% of total	1984	1985	1986	1987	1988	1989	% of total	1990	1991	1992	% of total
PRIMARY	4 144	1 193	677	5.9	8 820	4 174	3 068	10 021	127	1 571	2.3	3 454	−2 282	−1 215	−35.9
Agriculture	146	96	114	1.0	21	2	128	169	−86	74	0.1	−45	−114	−57	−1.7
Mining and quarrying	833	−1 292	53	0.5	1 683	320	1 150	1 259	2 262	639	0.9	2 836	523	720	21.3
Oil[1]	3 165	2 389	510	4.4	7 116	3 852	1 790	8 593	−2 049	858	1.2	663	−2 691	−1 878	−55.4
SECONDARY	7 455	2 629	3 686	32.0	4 363	8 911	14 107	25 022	31 924	38 604	55.9	17 053	8 276	4 039	119.2
Food, beverages and tobacco[2]	971	922	803	7.0	878	2 534	1 313	3 168	418	7 757	11.2	−897	1 331	2 096	61.9
Textiles, leather and clothing[3]	72	3	5	0.0	44	35	270	128	511	749	1.1	45	−196	−173	−5.1
Paper, printing and publishing	620	211	443	3.8	598	1 458	1 943	1 919	5 736	2 929	4.2	1 597	1 245	−282	−8.3
Chemical products	3 211	662	1 407	12.2	1 028	2 162	4 944	7 042	5 749	13 341	19.3	8 459	3 489	2 247	66.3
Coal and petroleum products	..	..	..	..	..	..	..	..	..	..	..	..	..	..	..
Non-metallic products[4]	−7	82	139	1.2	199	62	440	1 026	1 757	970	1.4	894	276	773	22.8
Metal products	878	−297	200	1.7	657	1 278	561	1 693	2 312	3 223	4.7	3 037	−821	231	6.8
Mechanical equipment	603	−49	−41	−0.4	255	231	306	1 419	4 446	3 374	4.9	307	649	−558	−16.5
Electric and electronic equipment	542	427	144	1.3	601	−137	2 711	2 658	1 647	4 446	6.4	271	1 347	−1 464	−43.2
Motor vehicles	−35	318	327	2.8	99	247	528	412	710	1 296	1.9	500	−10	−11	−0.3
Other transport equipment	72	173	−188	−1.6	9	61	−95	356	58	277	0.4	−198	212	75	2.2
Other manufacturing	528	177	447	3.9	−5	980	1 186	5 201	8 580	242	0.4	3 038	754	1 105	32.6
TERTIARY	13 446	9 988	7 155	62.1	12 384	7 405	18 970	24 539	26 519	28 836	41.8	27 914	19 452	564	16.6
Construction	2 626	529	7	0.1	538	107	−201	374	147	205	0.3	508	−229	−294	−8.7
Wholesale and retail trade	4 794	3 102	2 663	23.1	3 907	4 421	6 272	7 728	7 334	2 980	4.3	7 769	4 136	−361	−10.7
Transport and storage	209	138	120	1.0	−56	179	358	136	610	191	0.3	583	16	−702	−20.7
Finance, insurance and business services	2 887	5 874	4 257	37.0	8 026	2 321	10 283	9 092	10 220	18 643	27.0	2 617	11 933	218	6.4
Communication	..	..	..	..	..	..	..	−44	−148	−1 319	−1.9	9	−8	270	8.0
Other services[5]	2 930	..	..	..	..	..	..	7 253	8 356	8 136	11.8	16 428	3 604	1 430	42.2
UNALLOCATED	150	..	..	..	..	..	..	..	..	..	..	..	..	..	..
TOTAL	25 195	13 810	11 518	100.0	25 567	20 490	36 145	59 582	58 570	69 011	100.0	48 421	25 446	33 88	100.0

1. Including petroleum manufacturing products and petroleum related services.
2. Excluding tobacco which appears under "Other manufacturing".
3. Excluding leather which appears under "Other manufacturing".
4. Including rubber and other plastic products.
5. Including real estate, hotels and restaurants, motion pictures, engineering, accounting and other services.
Source: United States Department of Commerce, Bureau of Economic Analysis: *Survey of Current Business*, various issues.

Chart 2. **Foreign direct investment flows by industry**

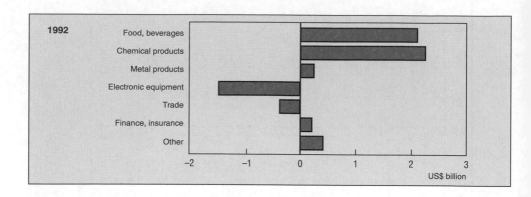

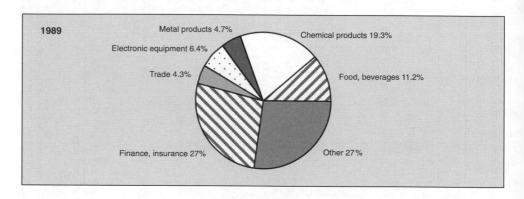

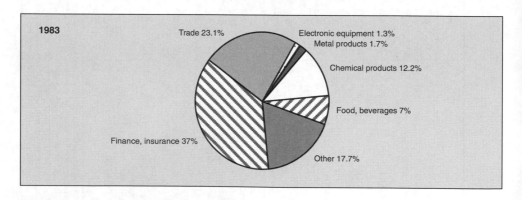

Source: US Department of Commerce Survey of Current Business.

Table 4.   **Estimated shares of non-bank affiliates of foreign companies
in selected US economic indicators**

In per cent

	1980	1987	1989	1990
Total US gross domestic product	2.6	3.5	4.3	4.6
All non-bank private industry:				
Gross domestic product	3.4	4.3	5.6	6.0ᵉ
Employment [1]	2.7	3.7	4.8	5.0
New plant and equipment expenditures [2]	5.5	7.6	10.4	12.2
R&D expenditures	6.4	10.6	13.4	15.4
Manufacturing industry [3] :				
Assets	8.3	13.2	17.6	18.6
Sales	7.1	11.4	15.2	16.4
Gross product	7.9	10.4	13.4	14.0ᵉ
R&D expenditures [4]	5.7	9.7	13.4	14.9
Total merchandise trade:				
Exports	23.1	18.9	23.7	23.2
Imports	30.9	35.3	36.3	36.5

e = estimated.
1.   Excludes employment in Puerto Rico, and in "other territories and offshore".
2.   Excludes agriculture.
3.   Based on industry of enterprise for affiliates and industry of establishment for all manufacturing.
4.   Petroleum and coal products manufacturing have been excluded because separate affiliate data for these industries are not available for 1986.
Note: Non-bank private industry gross product is total gross domestic product minus the gross product of banks, government and government enterprises, private households, imputed GDP of owner-occupied housing, rental income of persons, business transfer payments, subsidies, and the statistical discrepancy.
Source: US Department of Commerce, Bureau of Economic Analysis and Bureau of the Census; and the National Science Foundation

Industry	Affiliate employment (in thousands)			Share of US employment (in per cent)		
	1980	1987	1990	1980	1987	1990
All industries	2 034	3 224	4 705	2.7	3.7	5.0
Manufacturing	1 110	1 472	2 097	5.4	7.7	10.9
Petroleum and coal products	65	71	91	*	*	*
Chemicals	170	269	331	15.2	26.2	30.3
Stone, clay and glass	37	82	108	5.6	14.5	19.3
Electric and electronic equipment	161	202	274	7.6	12.0	16.2
Primary metals	64	90	112	5.6	12.2	14.8
Rubber and plastics products	38	57	121	5.3	6.6	13.5
Food	103	137	203	6.0	8.4	12.1
Instruments	52	76	109	7.4	7.4	10.9
Motor vehicles and equipment	59	56	87	7.4	6.6	10.6
Nonelectric machinery	115	122	217	4.6	5.9	10.3
Other manufacturing	41	47	51	5.5	7.9	8.6
Fabricated metals	52	58	103	3.2	4.1	7.2
Paper and allied products	35	46	50	5.1	6.9	7.1
Print and publishing	42	83	109	3.3	5.4	6.8
Textile mill products	21	27	37	2.5	3.7	5.3
Other transport equipment	22	12	42	2.0	1.0	3.5
Apparel and other textile products	11	12	27	0.8	1.1	2.6
Lumber, wood, furniture and fixtures	20	25	27	1.7	1.9	2.1
Mining	61	68	95	5.9	9.4	13.4
Transportation	40	87	223	1.3	2.7	6.2
Wholesale trade	147	282	348	2.7	4.7	5.5
Insurance	61	81	121	3.5	3.9	5.4
Retail trade	372	633	867	2.4	3.3	4.3
Finance, except banking	28	83	64	3.0	5.3	4.1
Real estate	17	31	37	1.5	2.2	2.5
Services [1]	109	329	645	0.6	1.3	2.2
Business services	25	159	268	0.8	3.0	5.0
Agriculture, forestry and fishing	14	18	33	0.8	1.0	1.8
Construction	43	57	70	1.0	1.1	1.3
Communication and public utilities	2	14	27	0.1	0.6	1.2
Unspecified	30	70	79			

* Affiliate and all US business data are not comparable. The 1990 share, when appropriate adjustments are made, is about 39 per cent.
1. Excludes private households.
Note: The affiliate data are classified by industry of sales. The all-US-business data used to calculate the ratios are on an industry-of-establishment basis. In this table, petroleum is not shown as a separate major industry. Instead, in order to be consistent with the all-US-business data, affiliate employment in the various petroleum categories is distributed among the other major industries. Thus, manufacturing includes petroleum and coal products, wholesale trade includes petroleum wholesale trade, retail trade includes gasoline service stations, and so on.
Because of changes in SIC codes, the industry coverage for 1980 differs somewhat from that for 1987 and 1990. The largest changes in the all-US data involve instruments and electrical equipment.
Based on establishment date for affiliates and all US business for 1987, it appears that the affiliate share of employment may actually be lower than these data indicate for chemicals manufacturing and higher than these data indicate for mining.
Source: US Department of Commerce, Bureau of Economic Analysis.

Table 6. **US Merchandise trade, total and by US affiliate and all other firms, 1980-1990**

Million US$

	Total US enterprises			US owned firms			US affiliate firms			US affiliate share		
	Exports	Imports	Balance	Exports	Imports	Balance	Exports	Imports	Balance	Exports (%)	Imports (%)	Balance (%)
1980	225.7	245.3	-19.5	173.5	169.5	4.1	52.2	75.8	-23.6	23.1	30.9	120.8
1981	238.7	261.0	-22.3	174.6	178.7	-4.1	64.1	82.3	-18.2	26.8	31.5	81.6
1982	216.4	244.0	-27.5	156.2	159.7	-3.5	60.2	84.3	-24.1	27.8	34.6	87.4
1983	205.6	258.0	-52.4	151.8	176.6	-24.8	53.9	81.5	-27.6	26.2	31.6	52.7
1984	224.0	330.7	-106.7	165.8	230.2	-64.4	58.2	100.5	-42.3	26.0	30.4	39.7
1985	218.8	336.5	-117.7	162.4	223.2	-60.8	56.4	113.3	-56.9	25.8	33.7	48.4
1986	227.2	365.4	-138.3	177.6	239.7	-62.1	49.6	125.7	-76.2	21.8	34.4	55.1
1987	254.1	406.2	-152.1	206.0	262.7	-56.7	48.1	143.5	-95.4	18.9	35.3	62.7
1988	322.4	441.0	-118.5	252.9	285.4	-32.5	69.5	155.5	-86.0	21.6	35.3	72.6
1989	363.8	473.2	-109.4	277.5	301.4	-23.9	86.3	171.8	-85.5	23.7	36.3	78.2
1990	393.6	495.3	-101.7	302.5	314.6	-12.2	91.1	180.7	-89.5	23.2	36.5	88.0

May not add due to rounding.
Source: Bureau of Economic Analysis.

Table 7. **US affiliate import dependence in 1990**

Average ratio of merchandise imports to sales

Type of US Affiliate	Per cent
All US Affiliates	15.5
By industry of US affiliates:	
Manufacturing	11.6
Motor vehicles and equipment	34.1
Other manufacturing	10.7
Wholesaling	29.7
Motor vehicles and equipment	48.5
Other wholesaling	23.6
By country of UBO:	
Japan	28.0
Other UBO	10.9

Source: Bureau of Economic Analysis.

Table 8. Direct investment flows abroad by country, 1981-1992

Million US$

	1982	1983	% of total	1984	1985	1986	1987	1988	1989	% of total	1990	1991	1992	% of total
OECD AREA	2 317	7 186	107.4	8 821	8 336	10 110	19 715	12 350	27 216	72.4	15 385	21 404	19 035	51.3
Europe	3 470	5 122	76.5	5 578	7 573	7 292	11 397	7 854	23 397	62.2	8 288	19 066	13 273	35.8
EEC	2 478	3 576	53.4	4 985	6 808	6 953	9 268	8 495	23 126	61.5	2 386	17 378	9 711	26.2
Belgium-Luxembourg	468	-62	-0.9	470	74	-357	967	1 077	734	2.0	549	1 330	713	1.9
France	76	155	2.3	177	944	394	1 008	1 663	1 584	4.2	1 053	2 092	2 836	7.6
Germany	370	632	9.4	357	213	1 070	644	1 873	2 522	6.7	1 464	6 133	1 571	4.2
Ireland	333	420	6.3	425	657	595	908	694	793	2.1	757	975	745	2.0
Italy	503	695	10.4	647	908	-615	811	391	1 657	4.4	1 152	1 540	922	2.5
Netherlands	-105	134	2.0	-118	569	3 304	2 000	615	3 112	8.3	-2 401	-2 355	-2 355	-6.3
Spain	-2	198	3.0	-23	247	444	492	436	979	2.6	391	-16	1 359	3.7
United Kingdom	754	1 385	20.7	3 052	3 147	2 259	2 559	4 170	11 825	31.5	-629	3 359	3 545	9.5
Other Europe	992	1 546	23.1	593	765	339	2 129	-641	271	0.7	5 902	1 688	3 562	9.6
Norway	265	264	3.9	-227	347	343	327	-1 083	-1 029	-2.7	-43	106	-147	-0.4
Switzerland	775	1 454	21.7	779	367	-4	1 802	410	1 269	3.4	5 284	897	2 997	8.1
North America	-1 690	878	13.1	3 260	76	2 491	6 099	2 653	1 268	3.4	3 471	1 164	3 257	8.8
Canada	-1 690	878	13.1	3 260	76	2 491	6 099	2 653	1 268	3.4	3 471	1 164	3 257	8.8
Other OECD Countries	537	1 186	17.7	-17	687	327	2 219	1 843	2 551	6.8	3 626	1 174	2 505	6.7
Australia	166	250	3.7	165	299	-46	981	687	1 997	5.3	678	1 071	1 335	3.6
Japan	306	999	14.9	-245	333	343	1 160	1 036	299	0.8	844	244	867	2.3
NON OECD AREA	-1 225	-494	-7.4	2 832	4 384	7 591	9 262	5 515	10 383	27.6	12 315	10 695	18 087	48.7
Africa	672	5	0.1	368	-118	-162	220	-592	-554	-1.5	-504	104	-1 045	-2.8
Latin America-Caribbean	-4 065	-2 996	-44.8	778	4 199	7 282	8 129	6 036	9 089	24.2	9 505	6 871	13 673	36.8
Argentina	163	-73	-1.1	67	2	274	-25	115	59	0.2	327	388	586	1.6
Brazil	1 208	-257	-3.8	434	134	261	911	2 189	3 014	8.0	772	845	2 484	6.7
Mexico	107	-640	-9.6	115	136	-446	310	670	1 652	4.4	1 868	2 305	1 261	3.4
Middle East	195	1 258	18.8	596	-74	73	237	-270	-473	-1.3	563	660	1 085	2.9
Israel	-102	15	0.2	126	122	-110	154	92	-33	-0.1	25	94	497	1.3
Saudi Arabia	-89	1 054	15.8	226	83	49	212	-345	56	0.1	366	204	353	1.0
South and East Asia	1 804	1 065	15.9	1 862	164	944	1 000	894	1 657	4.4	2 672	3 317	4 220	11.4
DAEs	683	399	6.0	842	-24	815	1 083	1 054	1 573	4.2	1 804	2 597	3 389	9.1
Hong Kong	283	341	5.1	335	18	691	280	567	465	1.2	265	420	1 856	5.0
Korea	-167	-122	-1.8	124	42	58	156	141	332	0.9	312	194	-140	-0.4
Singapore	42	83	1.2	199	2	193	179	191	165	0.4	481	1 127	1 097	3.0
Taiwan	66	70	1.0	99	-79	80	345	-105	177	0.5	209	429	154	0.4
Other Asia	1 121	666	10.0	1 020	188	129	-83	-160	84	0.2	868	720	831	2.2
Indonesia	1 004	474	7.1	932	220	37	-322	-138	-65	-0.2	659	608	656	1.8
Other Countries	169	174	2.6	-772	213	-546	-324	-553	664	1.8	79	-424	-224	-0.6
TOTAL	1 092	6 692	100.0	11 653	12 720	17 701	28 977	17 865	37 599	100.0	27 700	32 099	37 122	100.0

Source: United States Department of Commerce, Bureau of Economic Analysis; Survey of Current Business, various issues.

Chart 3.   **Direct investment flows abroad by country**

1992

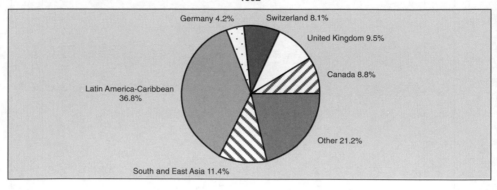

1989

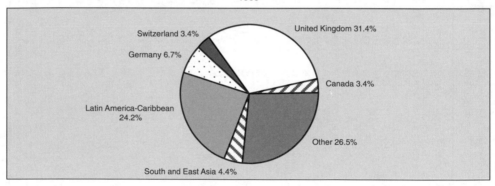

1983

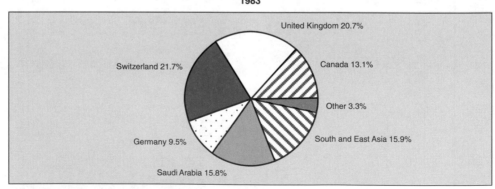

Source: US Department of Commerce Survey of Current Business.

Table 9. Direct investment flows abroad by industry, 1981-1992

in $ million

	1981	1982	1983	% of total	1984	1985	1986	1987	1988	1989	% of total	1990	1991	1992	% of total
PRIMARY	3 102	2 032	527	7.9	249	−1 617	1 417	1 461	−2 979	−6 966	−18.5	4 336	1 711	675	1.8
Agriculture	..	52	−32	−0.5	147	−246	−114	51	21	30	0.1	2	−19	51	0.1
Mining and quarrying	..	−1 855	86	1.3	−708	−158	−589	−945	−78	117	0.3	379	343	780	2.1
Oil [1]	3 102	3 835	473	7.1	810	−1 213	2 120	2 355	−2 922	−7 113	−18.9	3 955	1 387	−156	−0.4
SECONDARY	2 869	4 151	2 798	41.8	6 923	5 732	5 609	12 646	8 077	17 202	45.7	14 891	13 040	15 783	42.5
Food, beverages and tobacco [2]	..	793	492	7.4	1 087	840	1 161	761	405	−169	−0.4	5 937	2 149	2 358	6.4
Textiles, leather and clothing [3]	..	66	27	0.4	−146	47	−16	217	−23	100	0.3	106	75	294	0.8
Paper, printing and publishing	..	280	−166	−2.5	478	408	60	703	253	4 882	13.0	846	1 265	1 446	3.9
Chemical products	..	1 237	838	12.5	1 339	643	1 474	2 970	3 917	4 341	11.5	2 283	3 987	5 077	13.7
Coal and petroleum products	..	..	..	..	..	..	..	..	..	..	..	..	..	..	..
Non-metallic products	..	237	231	3.5	398	357	64	670	1 071	518	1.4	223	319	437	1.2
Metal products	..	−109	65	1.0	329	21	499	341	1 391	1 489	4.0	1 835	−454	750	2.0
Mechanical equipment	..	785	481	7.2	1 154	2 307	1 643	2 287	−173	1 200	3.2	1 219	1 112	−1 024	−2.8
Electric and electronic equipment	..	726	269	4.0	1 247	250	−1 520	934	437	2 917	7.8	1 151	263	1 184	3.2
Motor vehicles	..	−648	336	5.0	489	310	1 231	2 311	1 241	1 596	4.2	−705	2 253	3 574	9.6
Other transport equipment	..	−70	−39	−0.6	14	−33	216	55	−98	104	0.3	19	53	−10	0.0
Other manufacturing	2 869	854	264	3.9	534	582	797	1 397	−344	224	0.6	1 977	2 018	1 697	4.6
TERTIARY	3 652	−5 105	3 361	50.3	4 477	8 609	10 680	14 873	12 773	27 369	72.8	8 478	17 347	20 663	55.7
Construction	..	117	25	0.4	50	238	−65	−149	89	102	0.3	88	43	55	0.1
Wholesale and retail trade	..	−153	1 509	22.6	1 255	1 473	1 856	3 065	3 950	3 468	9.2	1 795	6 200	5 984	16.1
Transport and storage	..	−141	63	0.9	−162	136	203	−247	−24	286	0.8	330	412	489	1.3
Finance, insurance and business serv. [4]	..	−4 885	1 590	23.8	3 121	6 553	8 454	11 390	8 420	22 029	58.6	2 145	8 085	11 735	31.6
Communication		23	22	0.3	14	36	60	−77	30	146	0.4	2 455	1 422	1 068	2.9
Other services	3 652	−66	152	2.3	199	173	172	891	308	1 338	3.6	1 665	1 185	1 332	3.6
UNALLOCATED	..	..	..	..	..	..	..	..	..	..	..	..	..	..	..
TOTAL	9 623	1 078	6 686	100.0	11 649	12 724	17 706	28 980	17 871	37 605	100.0	27 705	32 098	37 121	100.0

1. Including petroleum manufacturing products and petroleum related services.
2. Excluding tobacco which appears under Other manufacturing.
3. Excluding leather which appears under Other manufacturing.
4. Excluding investment to the Netherlands Antilles.
Source: United States Department of Commerce, Bureau of Economic Analysis: Survey of Current Business, various issues.

Chart 4. **Direct investment flows abroad by industry**

1992

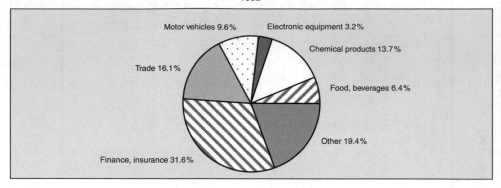

1989

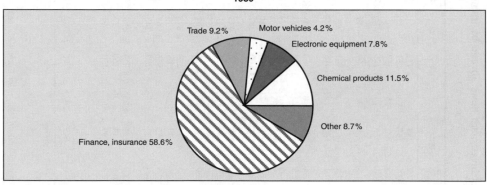

1983

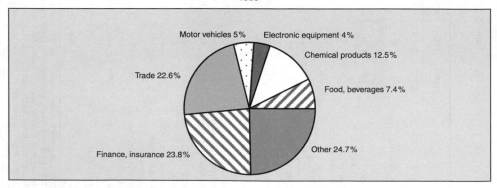

Source: OECD/DAF.

Annex 4

Statistics on direct investment flows in OECD countries

Table 1. **Foreign direct investment in OECD countries: inflows 1971-1993**[1]

US$ million

	Cumulative flows		Flows of foreign direct investment											
	1971-1980	1981-1990	1982	1983	1984	1985	1986	1987	1988	1989	1990	1991	1992	1993
Australia	11 295	40 369	2 286	2 994	428	2 099	3 457	3 873	7 936	7 887	7 060	4 904	5 286	2 460
Austria	1 455	3 274	207	219	116	169	181	402	437	578	647	359	940	982
Belgium-Luxembourg[2]	9 215	28 182	1 390	1 271	360	957	631	2 338	4 990	6 731	8 162	8 919	10 956	10 458
Canada[2]	5 534	33 699	−831	2 003	4 754	1 298	2 781	8 038	6 456	5 018	7 852	2 913	4 576	5 930
Denmark	1 561	3 388	136	64	9	109	161	88	504	1 084	1 133	1 530	1 015	1 684
Finland	376	2 838	−4	84	138	110	340	265	530	489	787	−247	396	593
France[2]	16 908	43 194	1 563	1 631	2 198	2 210	2 749	4 621	7 204	9 552	9 040	11 073	15 928	12 142
Germany	13 969	18 029	819	1 775	553	587	1 190	1 901	1 203	7 131	2 529	4 263	2 422	−286
Greece	..	6 145	436	439	485	447	471	683	907	752	1 005	1 135	1 144	977
Iceland[2]	..	12	..	..	14	23	8	2	−14	−27	6	35	17	..
Ireland	1 659	1 212	241	168	119	159	−43	89	91	85	99	97	102	88
Italy[2]	5 698	24 888	605	1 200	1 329	1 071	−21	4 144	6 882	2 181	6 344	2 481	3 210	3 751
Japan[2]	1 424	3 281	439	416	−10	642	226	1 165	−485	−1 054	1 753	1 368	2 728	86
Mexico	..	24 418	1 901	2 192	1 542	1 984	2 400	2 634	2 879	3 174	2 634	4 762	4 393	4 901
Netherlands	10 822	28 203	974	688	610	740	1 497	2 486	3 903	6 648	9 167	5 002	6 994	5 651
New Zealand	2 598	3 945	275	243	119	227	390	238	156	434	1 686	1 695	1 089	2 376
Norway	3 074	4 831	424	336	−210	−412	1 023	184	285	1 511	1 004	−291	720	2 058
Portugal[3]	535	6 918	145	150	194	273	241	465	925	1 740	2 608	2 451	1 914	1 311
Spain[2]	7 060	46 000	1 801	1 647	1 773	1 945	3 442	4 548	7 016	8 433	13 681	10 423	8 115	6 746
Sweden	897	8 612	361	223	290	206	1 079	646	1 661	1 809	1 965	6 322	−139	3 786
Switzerland	..	12 432	..	286	520	1 050	1 778	2 044	42	2 254	4 458	2 613	411	64
Turkey[4]	228	2 340	55	46	113	99	125	106	354	663	684	810	844	1 016
United Kingdom	40 503	130 469	5 286	5 132	−241	5 780	8 557	15 450	21 356	30 369	32 889	15 826	16 448	14 536
United States	56 276	359 650	12 464	10 458	24 748	20 010	35 623	58 219	57 279	67 737	47 916	26 086	9 888	21 366
TOTAL	188 249	836 329	30 973	33 665	39 951	41 973	68 286	114 629	132 497	165 179	165 109	114 529	99 397	102 676

1. Data updated in May 1995. Including data for Mexico who became a Member of OECD on 18 May 1994.
2. Reinvested earnings are not included in national statistics.
3. Figures for Portugal are only available from 1975 onward.
4. Cumulated inflows since 1954.
Source: OECD/DAF – Based on official national statistics from the balance of payments converted in US$ at daily average exchange rate.

Table 2. Foreign direct investment in OECD countries: inflows 1982-1993[1]

As a percentage of GDP

	1982	1983	1984	1985	1986	1987	1988	1989	1990	1991	1992	1993
Australia	1.4	1.8	0.2	1.3	2.1	2.0	3.2	2.7	2.3	1.6	1.7	0.9
Austria	0.3	0.3	0.2	0.3	0.2	0.3	0.3	0.5	0.4	0.2	0.5	0.5
Belgium-Luxembourg[2]	1.6	1.5	0.4	1.1	0.5	1.6	3.2	4.2	4.1	4.3	4.7	4.9
Canada[2]	−0.3	0.1	0.4	−0.6	0.3	0.8	0.7	0.3	1.2	1.1	0.9	1.1
Denmark	0.2	0.1	0.0	0.2	0.2	0.1	0.5	1.0	0.9	1.2	0.7	1.2
Finland	0.0	0.2	0.3	0.2	0.5	0.3	0.5	0.4	0.6	−0.2	0.4	0.7
France[2]	0.3	0.3	0.4	0.4	0.4	0.5	0.7	1.0	0.8	0.9	1.2	1.0
Germany	0.1	0.3	0.1	0.1	0.1	0.2	0.1	0.6	0.2	0.3	0.1	0.0
Greece	1.1	1.3	1.4	1.3	1.2	1.5	1.7	1.4	1.5	1.6	1.5	1.3
Iceland[2]	0.0	0.0	0.5	0.8	0.2	0.0	−0.2	−0.5	0.1	0.5	0.3	0.0
Ireland	1.3	0.9	0.7	0.8	−0.2	0.3	0.3	0.2	0.2	0.2	0.2	0.2
Italy[2]	0.2	0.3	0.3	0.3	−0.0	0.5	0.8	0.3	0.6	0.2	0.3	0.4
Japan[2]	0.0	0.0	−0.0	0.0	0.0	0.0	−0.0	−0.0	0.1	0.0	0.1	0.0
Mexico	1.9	1.8	1.0	1.9	2.8	3.0	1.7	1.7	1.1	1.7	1.3	1.4
Netherlands	0.7	0.6	0.5	0.5	1.0	1.1	1.8	2.8	3.1	1.7	1.8	1.8
New Zealand	1.2	1.0	0.5	1.0	1.4	0.7	0.4	1.0	3.9	4.0	2.6	5.9
Norway	0.8	0.6	−0.4	−0.7	1.5	0.2	0.3	1.7	1.0	−0.3	0.6	2.0
Portugal	0.6	0.7	0.9	1.1	0.6	1.0	1.7	3.5	4.3	4.6	3.6	1.5
Spain[2]	1.0	1.0	1.1	1.2	1.5	1.6	2.0	2.2	2.8	2.0	1.4	1.5
Sweden	0.4	0.2	0.3	0.4	0.8	0.4	0.9	0.9	0.9	2.6	0.1	2.0
Switzerland	0.0	0.3	0.6	1.1	1.3	1.2	0.0	1.3	2.0	1.1	0.2	0.0
Turkey	0.1	0.1	0.2	0.2	0.2	0.2	0.5	0.8	0.6	0.7	0.8	0.2
United Kingdom	1.1	1.1	−0.1	1.3	1.5	2.2	2.6	3.6	3.4	1.6	1.7	1.5
United States	0.4	0.3	0.7	0.5	0.9	1.3	1.2	1.3	0.9	0.5	0.1	0.3

1. Data updated in May 1995. Including data for Mexico who became a Member of OECD on 18 May 1994.
2. Reinvested earnings are not included in national statistics.
Source: OECD/DAF – Based on official national statistics from the balance of payments.

Table 3. Direct investment abroad from OECD countries: outflows 1971-1993[1]

US$ million

	Cumulative flows		Flows of direct investment abroad											
	1971-1980	1981-1990	1982	1983	1984	1985	1986	1987	1988	1989	1990	1991	1992	1993
Australia	2 510	22 261	693	518	1 402	1 887	3 419	5 096	4 985	3 267	260	3 105	41	900
Austria	578	4 132	142	190	68	74	313	312	309	855	1 663	1 288	1 871	1 404
Belgium-Luxembourg[2]	3 213	21 454	−77	358	282	231	1 627	2 680	3 609	6 114	6 600	6 062	10 953	11 409
Canada[2]	11 335	41 847	709	2 633	3 685	3 862	3 501	8 538	3 848	4 583	4 732	5 856	3 688	7 176
Denmark	1 063	6 292	77	159	93	303	646	618	719	2 027	1 509	1 851	2 225	1 379
Finland	605	12 132	85	143	493	352	810	1 141	2 608	3 108	3 263	1 049	406	1 831
France[2]	13 940	85 618	3 063	1 841	2 126	2 226	5 230	8 704	12 756	18 137	26 920	20 501	19 097	12 167
Germany	24 846	86 573	2 481	3 170	4 389	4 804	9 616	9 105	11 431	14 549	23 168	22 879	17 745	11 673
Iceland[2]	..	27	..	..	..	..	2	7	1	8	9	10	27	..
Italy[2]	3 597	28 707	1 025	2 133	2 012	1 820	2 652	2 339	5 554	2 135	7 612	7 326	5 948	7 231
Japan[2]	18 052	185 826	4 540	3 612	5 965	6 452	14 480	19 519	34 210	44 130	48 024	30 726	17 222	13 714
Netherlands	27 829	52 940	2 582	2 267	2 392	2 847	3 021	6 954	4 422	11 373	13 589	12 270	14 096	10 079
New Zealand	375	4 563	87	404	31	174	87	562	615	135	2 365	1 472	391	−1 455
Norway	1 079	8 995	317	360	612	1 228	1 605	890	968	1 352	1 478	1 840	434	885
Portugal[3]	21	374	9	17	8	15	−2	−16	77	85	165	474	687	148
Spain[2]	1 274	8 196	505	245	249	252	377	754	1 227	1 470	2 845	3 574	1 273	2 599
Sweden	4 597	47 820	1 237	1 459	1 506	1 783	3 947	4 789	7 468	10 189	14 588	7 008	237	1 328
Switzerland	..	31 858	..	492	1 139	4 572	1 461	1 274	8 696	7 852	6 372	6 543	5 673	6 539
Turkey[4]	..	−7	..	..	..	..	..	9	-	-	−16	27	133	175
United Kingdom	55 112	185 674	7 145	8 211	8 039	10 818	17 077	31 308	37 110	35 172	18 729	15 597	19 444	25 697
United States	134 354	170 041	4 675	4 889	10 948	13 401	17 089	27 182	15 448	36 835	29 950	31 294	41 004	57 871
TOTAL	302 306	1 005 323	29 295	33 101	45 439	57 101	86 958	131 765	156 061	203 376	213 825	180 752	162 595	172 750

1. Data updated in May 1995. No data available on outflows for Mexico.
2. Reinvested earnings are not included in national statistics.
3. Figures for Portugal are only available from 1975 onward.
4. Includes cumulative investment since 1954.

Source: OECD/DAF – Based on official national statistics from the balance of payments converted in US$ at daily average exchange rate.

Table 4. **Direct investment abroad from OECD countries: outflows 1982-1993[1]**

As a percentage of GDP

	1982	1983	1984	1985	1986	1987	1988	1989	1990	1991	1992	1993
Australia	0.4	0.3	0.8	1.2	2.0	2.6	2.0	1.2	0.3	0.7	-0.1	0.3
Austria	0.2	0.3	0.1	0.3	0.3	0.3	0.2	0.7	1.0	0.8	1.0	0.8
Belgium-Luxembourg[2]	-0.1	0.4	0.4	0.3	1.4	1.8	2.3	3.8	3.3	2.9	4.7	1.9
Canada[2]	0.2	0.8	0.7	0.8	1.1	1.7	1.1	0.8	0.7	0.9	0.7	1.3
Denmark	0.1	0.3	0.2	0.5	0.8	0.6	0.7	1.9	1.2	1.4	1.6	1.0
Finland	0.2	0.3	1.0	0.7	1.2	1.3	2.5	2.7	2.4	0.9	0.4	2.2
France[2]	0.6	0.4	0.4	0.4	0.7	1.0	1.3	1.9	2.3	1.7	1.4	1.0
Germany	0.4	0.5	0.7	0.4	1.1	0.8	1.0	1.2	1.5	1.4	1.0	0.6
Iceland[2]	0.0	0.0	0.0	0.8	0.1	0.1	0.0	0.1	0.1	0.2	0.4	0.0
Italy[2]	0.3	0.5	0.5	0.4	0.4	0.3	0.7	0.2	0.7	0.6	0.5	0.7
Japan[2]	0.4	0.3	0.5	0.5	0.7	0.8	1.2	1.5	1.6	0.9	0.5	0.3
Netherlands	1.9	1.5	2.0	2.2	1.8	3.3	1.8	5.0	4.7	4.1	4.0	3.3
New Zealand	0.4	1.7	0.1	0.8	0.3	1.5	1.4	0.3	5.4	3.5	0.9	-2.8
Norway	0.6	0.7	1.1	2.1	2.3	1.1	1.1	1.5	1.4	1.7	0.4	0.9
Portugal	0.0	0.1	0.0	0.1	0.0	-0.0	0.2	0.2	0.3	0.7	0.9	0.2
Spain[2]	0.3	0.2	0.2	0.2	0.2	0.3	0.4	0.4	0.6	0.7	0.2	0.5
Sweden	1.2	1.6	1.6	1.8	3.0	3.0	4.1	5.3	6.3	2.9	0.5	0.7
Switzerland	0.0	0.5	1.3	4.9	1.1	0.7	4.7	4.4	2.8	2.8	2.0	2.8
Turkey	0.0	0.0	0.0	0.0	0.0	0.0	0.0	0.0	0.0	0.0	0.1	0.0
United Kingdom	1.5	1.8	1.9	2.4	3.0	4.5	4.4	4.2	1.9	1.5	1.6	2.7
United States	0.0	0.2	0.3	0.3	0.4	0.6	0.4	0.7	0.5	0.6	0.6	0.9

1. Data updated in May 1995. No data available on outflows for Mexico.
2. Reinvested earnings are not included in national statistics.
Source: OECD/DAF – Based on official national statistics from the balance of payments.

MAIN SALES OUTLETS OF OECD PUBLICATIONS
PRINCIPAUX POINTS DE VENTE DES PUBLICATIONS DE L'OCDE

ARGENTINA – ARGENTINE
Carlos Hirsch S.R.L.
Galería Güemes, Florida 165, 4° Piso
1333 Buenos Aires   Tel. (1) 331.1787 y 331.2391
Telefax: (1) 331.1787

AUSTRALIA – AUSTRALIE
D.A. Information Services
648 Whitehorse Road, P.O.B 163
Mitcham, Victoria 3132   Tel. (03) 873.4411
Telefax: (03) 873.5679

AUSTRIA – AUTRICHE
Gerold & Co.
Graben 31
Wien I   Tel. (0222) 533.50.14
Telefax: (0222) 512.47.31.29

BELGIUM – BELGIQUE
Jean De Lannoy
Avenue du Roi 202
B-1060 Bruxelles   Tel. (02) 538.51.69/538.08.41
Telefax: (02) 538.08.41

CANADA
Renouf Publishing Company Ltd.
1294 Algoma Road
Ottawa, ON K1B 3W8   Tel. (613) 741.4333
Telefax: (613) 741.5439
Stores:
61 Sparks Street
Ottawa, ON K1P 5R1   Tel. (613) 238.8985
211 Yonge Street
Toronto, ON M5B 1M4   Tel. (416) 363.3171
Telefax: (416)363.59.63

Les Éditions La Liberté Inc.
3020 Chemin Sainte-Foy
Sainte-Foy, PQ G1X 3V6   Tel. (418) 658.3763
Telefax: (418) 658.3763

Federal Publications Inc.
165 University Avenue, Suite 701
Toronto, ON M5H 3B8   Tel. (416) 860.1611
Telefax: (416) 860.1608

Les Publications Fédérales
1185 Université
Montréal, QC H3B 3A7   Tel. (514) 954.1633
Telefax: (514) 954.1635

CHINA – CHINE
China National Publications Import
Export Corporation (CNPIEC)
16 Gongti E. Road, Chaoyang District
P.O. Box 88 or 50
Beijing 100704 PR   Tel. (01) 506.6688
Telefax: (01) 506.3101

CHINESE TAIPEI – TAIPEI CHINOIS
Good Faith Worldwide Int'l. Co. Ltd.
9th Floor, No. 118, Sec. 2
Chung Hsiao E. Road
Taipei   Tel. (02) 391.7396/391.7397
Telefax: (02) 394.9176

CZECH REPUBLIC – RÉPUBLIQUE TCHÈQUE
Artia Pegas Press Ltd.
Narodni Trida 25
POB 825
111 21 Praha 1   Tel. 26.65.68
Telefax: 26.20.81

DENMARK – DANEMARK
Munksgaard Book and Subscription Service
35, Nørre Søgade, P.O. Box 2148
DK-1016 København K   Tel. (33) 12.85.70
Telefax: (33) 12.93.87

EGYPT – ÉGYPTE
Middle East Observer
41 Sherif Street
Cairo   Tel. 392.6919
Telefax: 360-6804

FINLAND – FINLANDE
Akateeminen Kirjakauppa
Keskuskatu 1, P.O. Box 128
00100 Helsinki
Subscription Services/Agence d'abonnements :
P.O. Box 23
00371 Helsinki   Tel. (358 0) 12141
Telefax: (358 0) 121.4450

FRANCE
OECD/OCDE
Mail Orders/Commandes par correspondance:
2, rue André-Pascal
75775 Paris Cedex 16   Tel. (33-1) 45.24.82.00
Telefax: (33-1) 49.10.42.76
Telex: 640048 OCDE

Orders via Minitel, France only/
Commandes par Minitel, France exclusivement :
36 15 OCDE

OECD Bookshop/Librairie de l'OCDE :
33, rue Octave-Feuillet
75016 Paris   Tel. (33-1) 45.24.81.81
(33-1) 45.24.81.67

Documentation Française
29, quai Voltaire
75007 Paris   Tel. 40.15.70.00

Gibert Jeune (Droit-Économie)
6, place Saint-Michel
75006 Paris   Tel. 43.25.91.19

Librairie du Commerce International
10, avenue d'Iéna
75016 Paris   Tel. 40.73.34.60

Librairie Dunod
Université Paris-Dauphine
Place du Maréchal de Lattre de Tassigny
75016 Paris   Tel. (1) 44.05.40.13

Librairie Lavoisier
11, rue Lavoisier
75008 Paris   Tel. 42.65.39.95

Librairie L.G.D.J. - Montchrestien
20, rue Soufflot
75005 Paris   Tel. 46.33.89.85

Librairie des Sciences Politiques
30, rue Saint-Guillaume
75007 Paris   Tel. 45.48.36.02

P.U.F.
49, boulevard Saint-Michel
75005 Paris   Tel. 43.25.83.40

Librairie de l'Université
12a, rue Nazareth
13100 Aix-en-Provence   Tel. (16) 42.26.18.08

Documentation Française
165, rue Garibaldi
69003 Lyon   Tel. (16) 78.63.32.23

Librairie Decitre
29, place Bellecour
69002 Lyon   Tel. (16) 72.40.54.54

Librairie Sauramps
Le Triangle
34967 Montpellier Cedex 2 Tel. (16) 67.58.85.15
Tekefax: (16) 67.58.27.36

GERMANY – ALLEMAGNE
OECD Publications and Information Centre
August-Bebel-Allee 6
D-53175 Bonn   Tel. (0228) 959.120
Telefax: (0228) 959.12.17

GREECE – GRÈCE
Librairie Kauffmann
Mavrokordatou 9
106 78 Athens   Tel. (01) 32.55.321
Telefax: (01) 32.30.320

HONG-KONG
Swindon Book Co. Ltd.
Astoria Bldg. 3F
34 Ashley Road, Tsimshatsui
Kowloon, Hong Kong   Tel. 2376.2062
Telefax: 2376.0685

HUNGARY – HONGRIE
Euro Info Service
Margitsziget, Európa Ház
1138 Budapest   Tel. (1) 111.62.16
Telefax: (1) 111.60.61

ICELAND – ISLANDE
Mál Mog Menning
Laugavegi 18, Pósthólf 392
121 Reykjavik   Tel. (1) 552.4240
Telefax: (1) 562.3523

INDIA – INDE
Oxford Book and Stationery Co.
Scindia House
New Delhi 110001   Tel. (11) 331.5896/5308
Telefax: (11) 332.5993

17 Park Street
Calcutta 700016   Tel. 240832

INDONESIA – INDONÉSIE
Pdii-Lipi
P.O. Box 4298
Jakarta 12042   Tel. (21) 573.34.67
Telefax: (21) 573.34.67

IRELAND – IRLANDE
Government Supplies Agency
Publications Section
4/5 Harcourt Road
Dublin 2   Tel. 661.31.11
Telefax: 475.27.60

ISRAEL
Praedicta
5 Shatner Street
P.O. Box 34030
Jerusalem 91430   Tel. (2) 52.84.90/1/2
Telefax: (2) 52.84.93

R.O.Y. International
P.O. Box 13056
Tel Aviv 61130   Tel. (3) 49.61.08
Telefax: (3) 544.60.39

Palestinian Authority/Middle East:
INDEX Information Services
P.O.B. 19502
Jerusalem   Tel. (2) 27.12.19
Telefax: (2) 27.16.34

ITALY – ITALIE
Libreria Commissionaria Sansoni
Via Duca di Calabria 1/1
50125 Firenze   Tel. (055) 64.54.15
Telefax: (055) 64.12.57

Via Bartolini 29
20155 Milano   Tel. (02) 36.50.83

Editrice e Libreria Herder
Piazza Montecitorio 120
00186 Roma   Tel. 679.46.28
Telefax: 678.47.51

Libreria Hoepli
Via Hoepli 5
20121 Milano   Tel. (02) 86.54.46
Telefax: (02) 805.28.86

Libreria Scientifica
Dott. Lucio de Biasio 'Aeiou'
Via Coronelli, 6
20146 Milano   Tel. (02) 48.95.45.52
Telefax: (02) 48.95.45.48

JAPAN – JAPON
OECD Publications and Information Centre
Landic Akasaka Building
2-3-4 Akasaka, Minato-ku
Tokyo 107   Tel. (81.3) 3586.2016
Telefax: (81.3) 3584.7929

KOREA – CORÉE
Kyobo Book Centre Co. Ltd.
P.O. Box 1658, Kwang Hwa Moon
Seoul   Tel. 730.78.91
Telefax: 735.00.30

MALAYSIA – MALAISIE
University of Malaya Bookshop
University of Malaya
P.O. Box 1127, Jalan Pantai Baru
59700 Kuala Lumpur
Malaysia   Tel. 756.5000/756.5425
                                         Telefax: 756.3246

MEXICO – MEXIQUE
Revistas y Periodicos Internacionales S.A. de C.V.
Florencia 57 - 1004
Mexico, D.F. 06600   Tel. 207.81.00
                                         Telefax: 208.39.79

NETHERLANDS – PAYS-BAS
SDU Uitgeverij Plantijnstraat
Externe Fondsen
Postbus 20014
2500 EA's-Gravenhage   Tel. (070) 37.89.880
Voor bestellingen: Telefax: (070) 34.75.778

**NEW ZEALAND
NOUVELLE-ZÉLANDE**
Legislation Services
P.O. Box 12418
Thorndon, Wellington   Tel. (04) 496.5652
                                         Telefax: (04) 496.5698

NORWAY – NORVÈGE
Narvesen Info Center – NIC
Bertrand Narvesens vei 2
P.O. Box 6125 Etterstad
0602 Oslo 6   Tel. (022) 57.33.00
                                         Telefax: (022) 68.19.01

PAKISTAN
Mirza Book Agency
65 Shahrah Quaid-E-Azam
Lahore 54000   Tel. (42) 353.601
                                         Telefax: (42) 231.730

PHILIPPINE – PHILIPPINES
International Book Center
5th Floor, Filipinas Life Bldg.
Ayala Avenue
Metro Manila   Tel. 81.96.76
                                   Telex 23312 RHP PH

PORTUGAL
Livraria Portugal
Rua do Carmo 70-74
Apart. 2681
1200 Lisboa   Tel. (01) 347.49.82/5
                                         Telefax: (01) 347.02.64

SINGAPORE – SINGAPOUR
Gower Asia Pacific Pte Ltd.
Golden Wheel Building
41, Kallang Pudding Road, No. 04-03
Singapore 1334   Tel. 741.5166
                                         Telefax: 742.9356

SPAIN – ESPAGNE
Mundi-Prensa Libros S.A.
Castelló 37, Apartado 1223
Madrid 28001   Tel. (91) 431.33.99
                                         Telefax: (91) 575.39.98

Libreria Internacional AEDOS
Consejo de Ciento 391
08009 – Barcelona   Tel. (93) 488.30.09
                                   Telefax: (93) 487.76.59

Llibreria de la Generalitat
Palau Moja
Rambla dels Estudis, 118
08002 – Barcelona
                 (Subscripcions) Tel. (93) 318.80.12
                 (Publicacions) Tel. (93) 302.67.23
                                   Telefax: (93) 412.18.54

SRI LANKA
Centre for Policy Research
c/o Colombo Agencies Ltd.
No. 300-304, Galle Road
Colombo 3   Tel. (1) 574240, 573551-2
                                   Telefax: (1) 575394, 510711

SWEDEN – SUÈDE
Fritzes Customer Service
S–106 47 Stockholm   Tel. (08) 690.90.90
                                   Telefax: (08) 20.50.21

Subscription Agency/Agence d'abonnements :
Wennergren-Williams Info AB
P.O. Box 1305
171 25 Solna   Tel. (08) 705.97.50
                                   Telefax: (08) 27.00.71

SWITZERLAND – SUISSE
Maditec S.A. (Books and Periodicals - Livres
et périodiques)
Chemin des Palettes 4
Case postale 266
1020 Renens VD 1   Tel. (021) 635.08.65
                                   Telefax: (021) 635.07.80

Librairie Payot S.A.
4, place Pépinet
CP 3212
1002 Lausanne   Tel. (021) 341.33.47
                                   Telefax: (021) 341.33.45

Librairie Unilivres
6, rue de Candolle
1205 Genève   Tel. (022) 320.26.23
                                   Telefax: (022) 329.73.18

Subscription Agency/Agence d'abonnements :
Dynapresse Marketing S.A.
38 avenue Vibert
1227 Carouge   Tel. (022) 308.07.89
                                   Telefax: (022) 308.07.99

See also – Voir aussi :
OECD Publications and Information Centre
August-Bebel-Allee 6
D-53175 Bonn (Germany)   Tel. (0228) 959.120
                                   Telefax: (0228) 959.12.17

THAILAND – THAÏLANDE
Suksit Siam Co. Ltd.
113, 115 Fuang Nakhon Rd.
Opp. Wat Rajbopith
Bangkok 10200   Tel. (662) 225.9531/2
                                   Telefax: (662) 222.5188

TURKEY – TURQUIE
Kültür Yayinlari Is-Türk Ltd. Sti.
Atatürk Bulvari No. 191/Kat 13
Kavaklidere/Ankara   Tel. 428.11.40 Ext. 2458
Dolmabahce Cad. No. 29
Besiktas/Istanbul   Tel. 260.71.88
                                         Telex: 43482B

UNITED KINGDOM – ROYAUME-UNI
HMSO
Gen. enquiries   Tel. (071) 873 0011
Postal orders only:
P.O. Box 276, London SW8 5DT
Personal Callers HMSO Bookshop
49 High Holborn, London WC1V 6HB
                                   Telefax: (071) 873 8200
Branches at: Belfast, Birmingham, Bristol,
Edinburgh, Manchester

UNITED STATES – ÉTATS-UNIS
OECD Publications and Information Center
2001 L Street N.W., Suite 650
Washington, D.C. 20036-4910 Tel. (202) 785.6323
                                   Telefax: (202) 785.0350

VENEZUELA
Libreria del Este
Avda F. Miranda 52, Aptdo. 60337
Edificio Galipán
Caracas 106   Tel. 951.1705/951.2307/951.1297
                                 Telegram: Libreste Caracas

Subscription to OECD periodicals may also be
placed through main subscription agencies.

Les abonnements aux publications périodiques de
l'OCDE peuvent être souscrits auprès des
principales agences d'abonnement.

Orders and inquiries from countries where Distribu-
tors have not yet been appointed should be sent to:
OECD Publications Service, 2 rue André-Pascal,
75775 Paris Cedex 16, France.

Les commandes provenant de pays où l'OCDE n'a
pas encore désigné de distributeur peuvent être
adressées à : OCDE, Service des Publications,
2, rue André-Pascal, 75775 Paris Cedex 16, France.

5-1995

OECD PUBLICATIONS, 2 rue André-Pascal, 75775 PARIS CEDEX 16
PRINTED IN FRANCE
(21 95 52 1) ISBN 92-64-14526-5 - No. 48043 1995
ISSN 1021-5794

OECD REVIEWS
OF FOREIGN
DIRECT INVESTMENT

UNITED STATES

ORGANISATION FOR ECONOMIC CO-OPERATION AND DEVELOPMENT

ORGANISATION FOR ECONOMIC CO-OPERATION AND DEVELOPMENT

Pursuant to Article 1 of the Convention signed in Paris on 14th December 1960, and which came into force on 30th September 1961, the Organisation for Economic Co-operation and Development (OECD) shall promote policies designed:

- to achieve the highest sustainable economic growth and employment and a rising standard of living in Member countries, while maintaining financial stability, and thus to contribute to the development of the world economy;
- to contribute to sound economic expansion in Member as well as non-member countries in the process of economic development; and
- to contribute to the expansion of world trade on a multilateral, non-discriminatory basis in accordance with international obligations.

The original Member countries of the OECD are Austria, Belgium, Canada, Denmark, France, Germany, Greece, Iceland, Ireland, Italy, Luxembourg, the Netherlands, Norway, Portugal, Spain, Sweden, Switzerland, Turkey, the United Kingdom and the United States. The following countries became Members subsequently through accession at the dates indicated hereafter: Japan (28th April 1964), Finland (28th January 1969), Australia (7th June 1971), New Zealand (29th May 1973) and Mexico (18th May 1994). The Commission of the European Communities takes part in the work of the OECD (Article 13 of the OECD Convention).

Publié en français sous le titre :
EXAMENS DE L'OCDE SUR L'INVESTISSEMENT DIRECT ÉTRANGER
ÉTATS-UNIS